QUOT-EBOS
ESSENTIAL – BARBS – OPINIONS – SAYINGS

CHARLES MWEWA

Copyright © 2020 Charles Mwewa

Published by:

AFRICA IN CANADA PRESS

Ottawa, Canada

All rights reserved.

ISBN: 978-1-988251-25-7

DEDICATION

To

Ngalula

R.I.P.

CONTENTS

DEDICATION iii

CONTENTS v

AUTHOR'S WORDS vii

1 | VISION 1

2 | KNOWLEDGE 21

3 | SECRETS 29

4 | CHARACTER & PERSEVERANCE 35

5 | JUSTICE, LAW & MORALITY 53

6 | FRIENDSHIP 67

7 | VALUE OF PAIN 73

8 | FAILURE GUARANTEE 75

9 | COVID-19 77

10 | BINARY QUANTUM 81

11 | RULE OF POWER 85

12 | GOVERNMENT & LEADERSHIP 89

13 | MONEY & WELBEING 103

14 | PERCEPTION 115

15 | MOTIVATION 117

16 | AFRICA & AMERICA 125

17 | VALUE OF THE PAST 127

18 | TRUST 129

19 | MASTERPIECE 131

20 | THE STONE OF GOLD 133

21 | POWER 135

22 | INSPIRATION 137

23 | LOVE AND FAMILY 149

24 | HOPE 179

25 | ACTIONS 191

26 | ANIMAL WISDOM 211

27 | MISCELLANOUS 217

ABOUT THE AUTHOR 297

AUTHOR'S CONTACT 299

INDEX 301

AUTHOR'S WORDS

I love thinking. I love wisdom. I love observing. There is nothing in the world that I do without involving my mind. Life is made up of patterns, designs and mental repetitions. Influence is relative, and throughout my life I have influenced people in my immediate circles in one way or the other. The quotes presented in this book have changed lives, livened dreams and recharged potentials.

Most, if not all, of them speak for themselves. They invigorate thoughts readers have already entertained. They rekindle mental forces readers have shunted. And they introduce new options of viewing life, endeavors, dreams and visions, experiences and skills and knowledge. At times, they challenge *status quo* and propose alternative approaches to life.

It is the hope of the author that the quotes contained in this book are not left to the vagaries of chance. On the contrary, the author's hope, in all humility, is that these quotes should be used to deliberately solve a life challenge, enhance potential, advance an endearing cause or draw the reader closer to their destiny or to good or to God.

Wisdom is the foundation of any good cause; it is the foundation of life itself. Wisdom is the basic ingredient of good leadership. Wisdom is grand; it is an attribute of divinity. It is a mark of excellence. And this book brings to you the ultimate *QUOTE* – *essential. barbs. opinions. sayings.*

Charles Mwewa
Ontario, Canada
September 2020

1 | VISION

1. "Visionary leadership is just stage one, eventually you have to alter from macro to micro management to accomplish goals."

2. "It is not what happens to you: Bad, ugly, awful, nauseating, repugnant, disappointing, embarrassing, frustrating, failing, losing, shaming, excoriating, humbling, abusive, stone-walling, belittling, demeaning, heartbreaking, defeating, and etc. It is not where you live: Poor, undeveloped, unhygienic, dirty, neglected, and etc. It is not who you are: Tall, short, fat, slim, African, European, American, Asian, Islander, educated, uneducated, learned or ignorant, young or old, male or female, exposed or local, married or divorced or single, and etc. It is not your tribe, your class, your culture, your language, your race, your caste, your position or lack thereof, your bank account or lack thereof, your status in the country, or etc. Not any one of these can bring you down and limit what you can do and be; if and when you decide to look above all

your negatives, they become wings to help you fly higher to your desired destiny."

3. "Leadership necessarily begins with vision, but results ultimately are dependent upon tangible actions."

4. "Vision is not only an industrial excellence; it is also a divine prerogative. God saw it before He made it."

5. "Leadership visioning is not presumption; you deliberately recreate the present with the eyes of the future."

6. "What you see in your mind, becomes easy to be accomplished in reality. That's vision."

7. "Almost all leadership begins with a vision."

8. "Vision gives you extra eye-view on operations, management, financing,

marketing, and etc., of your organization."

9. "Vision to leadership is the same as what a campus is to a Captain on a long and wide sea."

10. "Without a vision, leaders fail and followers fall."

11. "To drive you need sight; to reach a new destination, you need a new vision."

12. "Vision does not remove obstacles on the way; it only gives you courage to overcome them."

13. "99.9 percent of the times, a mission, a dream, a goal, an aim or an objective will falter if it's not watered in vision."

14. "Every road lead to somewhere; vision is the art of managing ends-in-mind."

15.: "Vision has many incisions."

16. "Draw, inscribe, diagram, plot, chart, and etc., the most important aspect of a vision is to see the end clearly."

17. "Presidents, Prime Ministers, leaders, ought to see their entire domains in one sight; directing is only possible if you can see."

18. "If you can't see it in your mind and feel it in your heart, it may not be fulfilled."

19. "Even blind people can have vision; so, there are no excuses."

20. "Vision can grow with exposure to further knowledge, experiences and observations."

21. "*Four Pillars of a Vision:* (1). Mindset - If your mind is not sold, you cannot buy your destiny. You must change your

mind to see and believe in the project you want to build. Read books, attend seminars, listen to experts, and etc.; (2) Skillset - If you have a right mindset without the right tools, you cannot build your project. Acquire the necessary skills needed to bring your vision to pass. Get training, etc.; (3) Build the Structure - Put the mindset and skillset in motion and erect the structure, mentally as well as physically; and (4) Build a System - Something that keeps on going irrespective of you, is a good system. It can run with or without you. At that point you know you have birthed an enduring vision to accomplish a project."

22. "Leadership vision and dream are interchangeably used; but vision is preferable, dreams may not come true, vision always does."

23. "Your vision must be bigger than your current resources and opportunities; if it's less, you are only a dreamer."

24. "You must see and talk about your vision as if it has already been fulfilled."

25. "What your vision sees, your hands do."

26. "If a vision fails, it's probably because the visionary is discouraged. If you keep holding on to vision, help will come."

27. "Refine, improve-upon, update, review, re-examine and expand on your vision, but don't give up."

28. "Tell what you see, that is how others catch what you have conceived. That's how vision expands."

29. "Dream of the whole universe, experience the world."

30. "You can't rise higher than what you see yourself in future."

31. "A constitution is not the vision of a nation, it's its structure; a leader's vision shapes the nation's future."

32. "A shepherd is a visionary, because he must first see where his flock will go."

33. "Reality may limit you, but vision expands you."

34. "As revealed, God never does anything He has not seen, for He calls things which be not as though they were."

35. "God never calls you to do something He hasn't seen you can do; life doesn't throw at you what you can't conquer."

36. "You can only see what you focus on, so is vision."

37. "The only thing that shortens distance between two positions, is vision,

otherwise you have to break the speed record."

38. "No matter how or where you were born, with a vision, you can rise higher than the mountains, and see all the possibilities."

39. "Eyes are the windows of the soul, and in dreams and visions, they come very much alive."

40. "A leader must have the knowledge to understand the competing options; the wisdom to make right and informed decisions; the courage to dispel criticisms; the flexibility to change; the faith to try new things; the grace to manage pressure; the confidence to lead; and a vision to accomplish."

41. "A true visionary leader identifies problems in order to solve them. And in solving them, a true leader separates people from the problem in order to fashion solution to the problem. Non-

leaders identify problems and blame them on the people, because non-leaders think of the people as a problem."

42. "In leadership, the purpose of the goal is more important than the size of it."

43. "A visionary leader may not be an expert in everything, but they must know what is going on in every department of the organization or obligation. Afterall, a leader owns both the successes and failures of their organization or obligation!"

44. "In any leadership arrangement, the people are divided into four categories of followers: Sheep; goats; cattle/bulls; and horses. With sheep, the leader leads from the front – trailblazing and guiding the way through example and care. With goats, the leader leads from all sides – because goats scamper from side to side. With cattle or bulls, the leader leads from the back – because going in front jeopardizes the leader's own wellbeing.

He may be trampled upon and killed. With horses, the leader mounts them and leads from the vertical – because the leader and the horse are of similar strength and wit."

45. "A leader is a teacher, first and foremost."

46. "*Speculation v. Anticipation*: In speculations things could be; in anticipation things might be."

47. "*Attraction v. Attitude*: In attraction, somehow I have magical power and things could be; in attitude, I believe I can do it."

48. "*Win-Win v. Win-Lose Attitude:* In win-win, such as in negotiations, mediations, conciliations, resource-mobilization, responsibility for failure, and success are linked; in win-lose-mentality, rescue effort-mentality, I don't care-mentality, half-heartedness, responsibility only for success, and success is the end."

49. "*Half-full v. Half-empty Attitude*: In half-full, you see things clearly, you pay attention to details, and you are character and principle-centred, fixed-goal-posts; In half-empty, you are in the state of 'ifs' where things are not clear, beginners-mentality, personality-centered, and shifting-goal-posts."

50. "No matter how many times you get knocked down, keep getting up as long as there is strength in you."

51. "When your mind comprehends something, your eyes will see it."

52. "Failure is looking at a problem in only one way, which is also wrong. There is more than one way of looking at a problem. Most of those ways will be right."

53. "The journey of one mile begins with a step. Similarly, the journey towards one million dollars begins with a penny."

54. "Perception is like a duck; calm on the surface but paddling underneath."

55. "Perception is giving people a positive impression of you. It is different from deception."

56. "As a leader, you are attracting people every day by the way you appear. It is your responsibility to know how you want people to perceive you."

57. "Most people who do much in life and change things have learned to 'refuse.' They refuse to give up; to be belittled, to be boxed in circles, to be stripped of purpose, to be cheated on their vision, to have their dreams die, to be used by others, to be defined by their limitations, to be confined to what they have, to be told what to do, to be shaped by their environment, to be forced to quit, to be

called 'losers,' to be shamed by past failures, to be trodden under by the devil, to be framed by their history, and to be told, 'You're not important.'"

58. "Only they who are capable of seeing their own back with their own eyes are not capable of being deceived."

59. "Unless you can see your own face with your own eyes, don't pass judgment on another."

60. "Help the people you need to help today; give to the people and causes you need to give to today; love the people around you today; care for things that matter more than today, today; and do, say and make the best things today. When it comes to life, nobody knows whether tomorrow will be yours, but you're sure of today – so become what you've intended to become today."

61. "When a person finds themselves doing what they should have done last year, (they are lucky to be alive this year) that's when it becomes failure."

62. "Itch not to hear a fellow human being has failed, but desire to help those who can't help themselves."

63. "Go, do, act, make and create are action words. Gone, done, made and created are completed action words. A deed, a creation and an action are nouns of something completed. Make your action word a noun at the end of the day."

64. "Failure is success when you did your best and your best was judged as not measuring up."

65. "In a world of over seven billion people and counting, it is foolishness to think that you can outwit everybody – it is sufficient to do what you can but just do it wholeheartedly."

66. "The happiest place on earth is where you are today, right now – eat, love, play and pray, and be merry; tomorrow, aim to be happier."

67. "If you think you are important because of your accomplishments, you will find out at two events: When people get old and no-one mentions what you did anymore (and another's work has overtaken it) and when you are dead (and no-one at your funeral seems to be impressed by what you did but only by who you were)."

68. "The most important thing in life is not a thing; it's called people."

69. "If people perish due to lack of vision, then the opposite is true, people can have life if they have something to live for."

70. "Risk-takers are history-makers - if you don't decide to do today, you will regret you never did yesterday. Leave

that leader who has been sucking your youth, energy and ideas out for his own agenda. Leave him, run far, it's better to fail trying to do your own thing than to succeed doing another man's vision."

71. "See the impossible possible before you can make the impossible into possibilities."

72. "The dream of changing the world starts in the mind."

73. "See what you want to become, and you will become."

74. "Anyone who loves sleep is a dreamer; visionaries dream wide awake."

75. "On the way to mission accomplishment, there stands many tenuous detours; the secret lies in not taking off your sight from the ultimate target."

76. "A person's greatest treasure is their cause in life."

77. "The simplest formula for influencing people is to attract them to you."

78. "The difference between leaders and followers is in the way they view the future. Leaders envision a future filled with possibilities while followers live by the moment."

79. "The Bemba people are the largest tribe in Zambia. In the olden times before the advent of modern system of transportation, like in most tribes in Africa, people relied on the word of mouth for direction and transmission of information. So, when you reached a particular village and asked about the route to your destination you were told that it was just by the big brown tree."

80. "Vision gives the person a sense of excitement even though the undertaking itself is overwhelming."

81. "Vision has the power in itself to produce actions that are necessary for the fulfilment of the vision."

82. "Without a vision, without a mental picture of an eminent future people perish. People who live for something have a greater chance to survive the storms of life. Those who live for nothing expire before their time."

83. "Where there is no vision, the people perish," (Proverbs 29:18, Bible).

84. "When an average, ordinary and natural person acquires a vision, it turns her into an above-average, extraordinary and supernatural conqueror."

85. "The glimpse rule of glory: God first shows you an inch of the mile He wants you to achieve. If you've experienced plenty, good health, happiness, favor or promotion before, you only experienced an inch of what you can achieve in future. A mile awaits. So, don't be discouraged if you are going through downs now, remember your past inch-glory, and you will achieve a mile-glory soon."

86. "Vision sees clearly in the dark, enjoys the fight when it is down, and becomes invincible when it is placed in a fix."

87. "The language of vision is the definition of tomorrow; what you see vividly before it is, you will become."

88. "The dark side of vision, is the bright side of action."

89. "A man with a vision has many lives but only dies once – those without, have only one life and do die many times over."

90. "Vision reaches further than naked eyes can see and is the link between substance and the metaphysical."

2 | KNOWLEDGE

1. "Seek knowledge even if you have to knock at the very entrance of Heaven."

2. "The earth is like a large pizza; you can only get a piece of it to the extent to which you know."

3. "You are defeated based on what you don't know; you succeed because of what you know."

4. "The mind is like a large ocean, no matter how many rivers of knowledge flow into it, it never gets filled."

5. "How can a boy born poor and a nobody change his destiny, by the knowledge of what is and what makes."

6. "If you want to make progress from where you are, simply know more than where you are."

7. "There is no monopoly of knowledge; you can find it in books, patches, nature and around you."

8. "God wants you to know more about everything, all things."

9. "Only what the brain knows gives rise to what your body does."

10. "Learn to know, and you have known the heart that beats in winners."

11. "There is no bigger problem than ignorance; if you don't know, you have a problem."

12. "There is no difference between ignorance and the grave, both kill potential."

13. "Know yourself first."

QUOT-EBOS

14. "The first knowledge you must pursue is to know what you are good at; then improve on it."

15. "It's better to improve on what you know than wasting time attending to what you don't know."

16. "To be a good teacher, you must know what your students know."

17. "To be a good student, you must aim at knowing what your teacher knows, and exceed it."

18. "The only thing that beats worry is knowledge."

19. "The only exam that you achieve zero percent in, is the one you did not take."

20. "You can't say you can be anything if you can't read about everything."

21. "Knowledge is like a bright light, wherever it shows up, the darkness of ignorance flees."

22. "The only reason you are where you are is because you don't know anything different."

23. "The knowledge of only one discipline is a curse; you only think from one perspective, your own."

24. "You can't think more than you know."

25. "You can't be more than you know."

26. "Ideas are brain children of knowledge, the less you know, the less ideas you have."

27. "To the ignorant, a hill is a mountain."

28. "Knowledge of what is, is sorrow, but knowledge of how to, is what brings gold out of an ore."

29. "The best way to know is to ask questions."

30. "Even faith is the substance of things hoped for; there is knowledge before there is faith."

31. "Faith comes by hearing, without knowledge, there is little chance for salvation."

32. "It is easier to confuse presumption with knowledge."

33. "Don't marry the person you don't know - it'll be like building a house from the roof."

34. "If what you are doing is not working for you, learn something new; it's never too late to change a profession."

35. "Most people think they don't love something; they just don't know it that well."

36. "You will always hate what you don't know very well, this includes your spouse."

37. "A fool says in his heart that there is no God; he's a fool because he doesn't know."

38. "Money doesn't make you rich; what makes you rich is the knowledge of how to make and keep money."

39. "The only thing that conquers the future is knowledge."

40. "You prayed about it, now know about it, and you will have your answer."

41. "The ignorant are the most abused, intimidated and impoverished people on earth."

42. "If the reason why you are where you are is because someone told you there

QUOT-EBOS

aren't better things elsewhere, they lied to you."

43. "The only reason why Africa sells itself to the West is because Africa doesn't know its value."

44. "A small heart has no love; a small mind lacks knowledge."

45. "Knowledge expands you in ways that makes you a jack of all trades and master of all."

46. "Don't follow a leader who doesn't give you a chance to know more than him."

47. "You can have sex with just about any person, but you can only make love with a person you know."

48. "You can only boast about the thing you know well."

49. "To be ruled by an ignorant leader is worse than falling into a ditch, it's falling into hell."

50. "The highest knowledge of oneself is when you begin to see that you're inadequate in yourself and you need a higher power to guide you."

51. "Don't be afraid to fail, to be rejected or to be disappointed, just know how to succeed, accept yourself and appoint yourself."

52. "If you don't know what they are saying, even if they say something good about you, you will not know."

53. "The more languages you know, the faster your brain works; why should UK with only English conquer Africa with so many languages?"

54. "Ignorance of the law is not a defence, so is ignorance of anything, it leaves you defenseless."

3 | SECRETS

1. "There is no revelation without secrets."

2. "There are certain things about you that only God should know."

3. "When people know your secrets, you become predictable; predictable people are expendable."

4. "Defend your secrets, the future of your destiny depends on them."

5. "Once a secret is known, the only thing that can restore it is war."

6. "A prostitute sells her body for sex; but she who reveals her secrets sells her soul for nothing."

7. "Once I know your name, date of birth and telephone or email, you're my slave."

8. "How did Europe conquer Africa, Europe first learned about Africa."

9. "Nations whose secrets are known to everybody, do not prosper."

10. "Some secrets are not meant to be revealed; they are meant to be concealed."

11. "If you can't keep a secret, you can't defend a city."

12. "No number of weapons and defence can save you from destruction, if your enemy knows your secrets."

13. "The only reason why you're in trouble is because they discovered your secret; if you keep a secret, no trouble will come!"

14. "With secrets, an empire becomes invincible!"

15. "The first thing your enemy will use to defeat you, is your secret!"

16. "Only give your secrets to a wise person; they will protect you in the day of calamity!"

17. "To whom you reveal all your secrets, from that person's hand you will fall!"

18. "Your secret is your last line of defence; if it falls, so does your guard!"

19. "Secrecy is an 11th commandment."

20. "What is the definition of foolishness? It is revealing what is to be a secret and keeping sealed what is to be opened."

21. "The secret that God doesn't want to reveal Himself to us physically, is a secret called faith."

22. "Dogs don't eat dogs; so, a wise person doesn't devour secrets."

23. "A leader is the one called to protect secrets."

24. "Your way to victory, progress and prosperity is a secret; if you discover it, it becomes your victory, progress and prosperity."

25. "Wars are won by secrets; but nations are governed because of secrets."

26. "Secrets are made for wise minds; foolishness is in the words of an open mouth."

27. "Don't tell your partner the truth about his/her sexual performance, tell them the truth of the future performance you desire."

28. "Although we are born naked, God does not want us to live naked."

29. "Truth is a weapon, and so is a secret!"

30. "Jesus is truth, and yet He was hidden in Scriptures."

31. "Only the truth that you can defend is worth revealing, everything else will lead to misunderstandings."

32. "Sometimes it is plain stupidity to tell someone the truth; if truth is used to destroy, it destroys indeed."

33. "Yes, there are some secrets you MUST hide from your spouse, if you expose

them carelessly, you may have murdered love."

34. "A secret is a powerful weapon; nations rise and fall to the extent to which their secrets are exposed."

35. "Do you know that God is in everything everywhere, but only those who seek Him will find Him?"

36. "If a woman exposes her agents of beauty so easily, she has lost value in the main."

37. "The reason why we hide our genitalia is because secrecy is more valuable than exposure."

38. "Jesus used more parables because they hide secrets."

39. "The purpose of a secret is to seek to revealing it; what is achieved by solving a secret is more valuable than what is direct."

40. "If the secret you hold will only hurt others and doesn't bring any benefit, do not share it with others."

41. "It is the glory of God to conceal a matter; to search out a matter is the glory of kings."[1]

42. "The secret things belong to the LORD our God, but the things revealed belong to us and to our children forever, so that we may follow all the words of this law.[2] O, the depth of the riches of the wisdom and knowledge of God."[3]

---

[1] Proverbs 25:2
[2] Deuteronomy 29:29
[3] Romans 11:33

4 | CHARACTER & PERSEVERANCE

1. "When you know that what you are doing is good, do not get tired doing it."

2. "Life is like a race; run yours without giving up."

3. "If things don't turn out fine the first time, try the second time."

4. "Perfection is a process, and not an event."

5. "Success is the closest exit to failure; just hang in there, you're almost arriving."

6. "If you think that you will not face trials, you're not ready for achievement."

7. "Almost everything that has value, takes fire or beating to become perfect."

8. "If you pass through hardships, you are on the right path to victory."

9. "You can do hard things, yes, you can."

10. "Persistence gives birth to mature character."

11. "If you give up, not even prayer can save you."

12. "At the center of every good character is self-respect."

13. "The more challenges you face, the surer you are to reaching your dreams."

14. "Good things are about to happen if you experience great resistance."

15. "Spring always comes after winter."

16. "The best lessons in life are learned from moments of weakness."

17. "If you laugh at a person who has failed, you are probably immature."

18. "You can realize your dream at any age, time or moment in life."

19. "When you lose one job, aim to get another – better paying, better conditions, better rewarding."

20. "The best miracles are those where you had no alternative."

21. "If you have nowhere else to lean to, lean on God."

22. "When you please God, he turns your defeat into a promotion."

23. "There are no failures in life; there are only people who fail to rise up when they fall."

24. "Guard your mind; if it is defeated, your energy is destroyed."

25. "Keep your dream alive, even if you die, your dream will be realized."

26. "Turn your disappointments into your appointments."

27. "The same fire that burns you, may also warm you up."

28. "The same water that quenches your thirst, may also drown you."

29. "The bitterest hell you experience, the sweetest heaven you will reap."

30. "From the darkest night, comes the brightest day."

31. "When people count you out; don't despair, count yourself in."

32. "Always defend yourself; God will stand with you."

33. "Death is not a punishment, but a joy to those who love God."

34. "A believer in God is undefeated; in life she wins, in death she wins."

35. "The best revenge in everything is not to do anything."

36. "Problems, troubles, discouragements, disappointments, distresses and oppositions are vehicles towards a destination called character."

37. "Any baby who remains in his mother's womb, shall never walk."

38. "Anything called an obstacle is good news, because behind it is what you want."

39. "Suffering is the breakfast champions feed on."

40. "The first quality you must display when you receive bad news is patience."

41. "Behind any promise is the promise to overcome any hindrances."

42. "Once you go through all the trials and challenges life throws at you, you will lack nothing."

43. "In every challenge there is a silver-lining, your job is to discern it."

44. "There is always pain through the birthing process."

45. "The most disheartening lie is to believe that your employment is your destiny."

46. "If your profession or career becomes your hindrance, change course."

47. "If you face moments of hopelessness, find something to encourage you."

48. "If you love God, everything against you is for you."

49. "If mercy or compassion is at the end of the road, don't be afraid to take that route."

50. "If you want to do ALL things, simply get into Christ."

51. "If you feel afraid, your enemy is fear."

52. "The greatest strength you have is to forgive those who wrong you."

53. "If your enemy wants to take your life, give him your love."

54. "The only discipline you should submit to, is the one resulting in good character, if it is in bad faith, fight it with all your might."

55. "Jesus said that there is trouble in the world; it's not me. But he also said that we should not be cheerless, because He has overcome the world. So, even trouble in the world works for our good."

56. "If your body refuses to dance, sing; if it refuses to sing, smile; and if it refuses to smile, praise."

57. "The first sin you commit is not to say something good about yourself."

58. "Behave well if there are witnesses around you."

59. "If what you believe in doesn't bring liberty, it is not faith; it is called religion."

60. "In everything you do in life, run as though you want to win, and you will win."

61. "When Satan betrayed God, God chased him away from Heaven; when you are betrayed, remove the betrayer far away from you."

62. "When ten voices are praising you, 90 others are waiting to trap you."

63. "If you are being tried, nothing unusual is happening to you."

64. "A godly lifestyle is lithe with trials, and only those who endure reach the aim."

65. "Philosophies and human traditions have power to enslave one, but knowledge of the higher power liberates."

66. "Only the truth that you know will set you free."

67. "You will make history if your disadvantages, weaknesses and misgivings become your assets for greatness."

68. "Do not despise your birth, upbringing, color of your skin, disabilities, height or weight, your name or your nationality."

69. "Do not look down or allow others to look down upon your past or present or future."

70. "Do yourself a favor, believe that history is made by people who did not have everything as demanded by society; it is made by those who, despite their own weaknesses, took on giant steps to silence all negative voices and move forward."

71. "The only thing that can stop you from reaching your highest mark is you."

72. "Adversity breakers are history makers."

73. "You are closest to success when you begin to feel like quitting."

74. "Failure is always temporary."

75. "Fall seven times and stand up eight" – Japanese proverb

76. "Like Albert Einstein, if you stay with the problem longer, you might just learn ways in which it does not work."

77. "When you fail, you can learn from it and begin again wisely, or you can yell over spilt milk."

78. "Prioritizing is the omen for achieving maximum in life without completing all your life."

79. "Change when you can, where you can and if you can."

80. "Success is the science of overlooking small failures and the art of not dwelling on big gains."

81. "A tortoise may complete the race as long as it does not stop going."

82. "You could lose all the battles and still win the war."

83. "Perseverance is the second job you get after you have planted your vision."

84. "Never count a man out if he has perseverance."

85. "The deeper the pangs of failure, the sweeter the taste of success."

86. "Find a job or make one."

87. "Join a business or create one."

88. "It always seems impossible until it's done," – Nelson Mandela

89. "A person's perspective can either be global or local; from either perspective, decisions are made which may have global or local consequences."

90. "Many times, the best decision to move forward is motivated by failure, intrigue or betrayal."

91. "Cherish every experience, especially the negative ones; the strike of iron that forges character is never immediately known."

92. "Reprimands, disappointments, disagreements, condemnations, vindictiveness, blame, mistakes, disloyalties, betrayals, or even failures and rejections, are all only temporary detours on the roadway towards mission accomplishment."

93. "The ability to receive, process and manage news of one's failures without fear or condemnation is one of the most revered characteristics visionary leaders are made of."

94. "Many know how to make merry and celebrate victory; but only a few fortunate ones know how to receive and process defeat."

95. "A perfectly prepared diet is a concoction of many tastes; some bitter, sour, sweet, salty, savory, spicy and pungent, umami and others vain, tasteless or flat and astringent. These tastes each lend a unique property and adduces a different benefit to the nutrition experience. A balanced mixture of these necessary tastes is at the heart and soul of any acclaimed culinary professional. Leadership is the same; all perspectives, both genders, all mixture of characters and their unique experiences matter. The bad, the good, the ugly, the beautiful, tricksters, purveyors, the subtle-minded, the smooth-talker and the lazy-bender, the witty and shrewdly, the thuggery and angelic, are all necessary to the aims of leadership. A wise leader knows when and how to balance all perspectives for a desired end. In this quest, a leader is like a surveyor – who prowls the end of the field to discover the gem, and then returns and bequeaths the knowledge, understanding, wisdom and secrets to the right professionals in order to reap the benefit stalked therewithin."

96. "With God, the bad intentions of your enemy can be the fertilizer that grows your destiny."

97. "Big victories are won with small defeats."[4]

98. "An enemy's biggest trick is friendship."[5]

99. "What Joseph's brothers meant for evil, God meant it for good."

100. "Right is always not wrong."

101. "A brother's betrayal stings like a warp but motivates like the warmth of the sun."

---

[4] Dervish Imam
[5] Ertugrul Bey

102. "Love is patient, love is kind. It does not envy, it does not boast, it is not proud. It is not rude, it is not self-seeking, it is not easily angered, it keeps no record of wrongs. Love does not delight in evil but rejoices with the truth."[6]

103. "Those who receive the greatest grace will suffer and experience pain the greatest."

104. "God's grace grows larger with more suffering."

105. "When the righteous experience pain and suffering, God's solution is the pouring out of more grace."

---

[6] 1 Corinthians 13:1

106. "The ultimate end of mature character is to display love, joy, peace, patience, kindness, goodness, faithfulness, gentleness, and self-control in all situations."

107. "Visionary eyes reach decisions without eyeglasses."

108. "Separation is necessary to growth, just like unity is essential to progress."

109. "Faith is that part of God that lives in us, enabling us to see beyond where our eyes can."

110. "Man sees obstacles as stumbling blocks; God views them as signposts of growth and character."

111. "A few brave soldiers can conquer a mountain; where many undisciplined cowards can fail to clear a hill."

112. "Love, and don't quit."

113. "Good character is a script that the future holds permanently; it continues to be played even when you are long gone."

114. "Character is fashioned from trouble, trials and hardships; perhaps no-one would grow if they never experienced peril."

115. "The hardest thing to do during life tests is also the noblest – to rejoice each time you encounter tough times."

116. "Character grows out of perseverance, just like a butterfly flies away from a chrysalis."

117. "Endurance may last but for a moment; the character therefrom produced lasts forever."

118. "The intrinsic value of perseverance manifests through the extrinsic worth of character."

5 | JUSTICE, LAW & MORALITY

1. "Laws are like people's undergarments; with good laws on, your comfort is secured though you may not realize it, and without them, shame is the end, though you may not know."

2. "Justice and law rarely leave each other. However, justice must always be a step ahead."

3. "Good laws are indispensable to good government; if the laws are bad, the good-willingness of the governors will not compensate."

4. "Law must be made indiscriminately, enforced impartially, and interpreted with divinity."

5. "If law is absent or weak, the devil in angels becomes a monster."

6. "Law must be a weapon – but for good and not revenge."

7. "Law is ultimately subservient to human dignity."

8. "Any government or public official who either debases law or uses it to disenfranchise others, has administered ricin into his own soul."

9. "Law must be just to be law."

10. "A decision-maker who makes a decision before hearing and weighing evidence objectively, has infected her own mind with poison ivy."

11. "Law is important – it can make a land fruitful or impotent."

12. "Law must constantly be reviewed to ensure that it does not defame the very ideals it purports to affirm."

13. "Law can be insipid, dumb or even stupid, but it can bite."

14. "Do not be proud to be a law-man, be happy to search and implement justice."

15. "To judge law, you must first judge yourself."

QUOT-EBOS

16. "For the most part, Justice is the person who sits on the bench to judge – if he lacks morality, you are presumed guilty."

17. "There is only one thing that is above the law, good evidence is."

18. "We continue to obey the law, even after we are dead."

19. "The only one who does not need law, is love."

20. "If you love the law, you probably hate evil."

21. "If you can bend the law, you can land into a ditch."

22. "No matter how justifiable it is, to condemn the innocent and to acquit the guilt, is shame to the law."

23. "Those who govern over other people, must govern by law."

24. "Good people respect the law; bad people disobey good laws."

25. "The law of the land must be strong in going to war against poverty, battling daily with corruption, and preaching democracy indefinitely."

26. "Those who make the law are not experts in the law – they must be beneath it."

27. "A good law must be immortal, invincible, incorruptible, and without guile."

28. "Law must not only defend the poor; it must bring them prosperity – because a good law must bring balance."

29. "If the law of the land fails to order society, either it is a useless law or those who enforce it are duplicitous."

30. "The first inherent nature of a good law is that it does not discriminate."

31. "Law to be effective, it must be allowed to govern those who govern."

QUOT-EBOS

32. "If the governors ignore the law, their judgments will be *anathema*."

33. "It is an abomination to allow law-breakers prosecute the law."

34. "Only the law made by God is holy, and the law made by good people is righteous."

35. "Law makes you to know sin but it does not tell you to sin."

36. "Law must be kept wholly."

37. "It is not law that tells you to do wrong to your neighbor."

38. "The surest way to show that you love your country, is by keeping its laws."

39. "Law has the right of life and death."

40. "A good law gives you the freedom to do good, a bad law rarely brings justice."

41. "Hitherto, only law and grace have been able to tame man's worst demons."

42. "The law of God is good, showing you the way."

43. "Law-abiding and lawlessness are like water and oil, they rarely mix."

44. "If you do what is right, you are not under the law."

45. "If you do evil, law will not spare you, even if you may hide in hell."

46. "The highest law of the land is the constitution; the highest law in nature is love."

47. "Conscience is the foundation of all laws."

48. "To be just, law must punish the wicked and reward the righteous."

49. "Justice is the ability to apply the law equally to all."

QUOT-EBOS

50. "Law demands absolute obedience; the law of relativity does not apply to law."

51. "No matter where they may have been born, all men are equal before and under the law."

52. "Bad men applying good laws, and good men applying bad laws, both inflict injury to conscience."

53. "What is injustice? It is using the law to exclude another and applying the law to satisfy your wicked intentions."

54. "Injustice, exclusionism, apartheid, racism, xenophobia, and similar-situated wrongs, are attributes of weak-minded depraved men."

55. "If you harbor any biases, no matter the degree or kind, you are disqualified from being a judge of men's affairs on earth."

56. "Right and wrong are the prerogatives of gods, men must search their consciences to discern between them."

57. "It is the curse of our century to tame human wrongs as human rights."

58. "If you call good bad, or bad good, you have no concept of justice."

59. "If you give the deserved what they don't deserve, or the underserved what they don't deserve, you have violated the first rule of morality."

60. "Those who govern, must govern with righteousness."

61. "If what you do or say will cause injury to the innocent, you are prejudiced."

62. "Collateral damage is a form of an injustice."

63. "No matter how you justify it, punishing the innocent is sin."

64. "There are three places where neither right nor wrong has any effect: Defending your loved ones; obeying God and carrying out a state mandate."

65. "No action is right or wrong, if that action is meant to win your spouse back."

66. "The first rule of justice is that everyone should receive what they deserve on the scale of rights and wrongs."

67. "You can't do justice without being just, righteous, equitable, morally right or fair."

68. "Equality and equity are the foundations of justice."

69. "Law and justice, both desires to establish state order and security."

70. "If citizens are no longer safe from their internal and external enemies, law and justice have failed."

71. "Do not suspend law, unless the benefits of so doing outweigh the danger that upholding the law prescribes."

72. "Whatever is not lawful is unlawful."

73. "Whatever is not just, is an injustice."

74. "A legal system that fails to defend the weak and put food in their mouth, is a laughing stock of the gods."

75. "It is immoral for a government to fail to provide food, shelter and comfort to its citizens; such a government has no credibility before God."

76. "A corrupt government should be removed, by any means possible."

77. "Life and death are in the palms of the governor, only righteousness and mercy can dictate otherwise."

78. "Betrayal is a greater sin, unless the betrayal is meant to uphold law and order."

79. "Death penalty is rarely the best way to punish injustice; it is an easy way."

QUOT-EBOS

80. "The law of men must be above men, but below the law of God."

81. "Poverty is against human rights."

82. "No-one should be denied justice in the name of order."

83. "When those who are entrusted with law and order are themselves corrupt, the people must do anything to restore justice."

84. "Civil disobedience is the righteous way of reordering society."

85. "When a government is above the law, the voice of the people must rule."

86. "Both thrones and judicial benches are set up for justice; only mercy may temper with judgment."

87. "It is not mercy if it acquits the evil and punishes the innocent."

88. "It is the law of justice that those who do wrong should be punished; of divine justice that a soul who sins shall die."

89. "Both the righteous and the wicked shall be judged; the former for rewards, the later to eternal damnation."

90. "Vengeance does not belong to men, but to God alone."

91. "A leader who maintains love and justice, pleases her maker."

92. "He who searches and reveals the deep things of darkness and brings utter darkness into the light, serves the purposes of God."

93. "Indeed, justice brings joy to the righteous but terror to evildoers."[7]

94. "'Eye for eye, and tooth for tooth,' is not a tool of justice but a convenience of vengeance."

95. "A good leader is the one who loves justice."

96. "Injustice is a characteristic of those who hate God."

97. "Justice is rarely fathomed by naked eyes; it takes the heart of wisdom to decipher it."

---

[7] Proverbs 21:15

98. "A people who allow justice and equity to prevail in the land, shall see many good years."

99. "Injustice favors favoritism; justice does not show partiality nor does it support those who pervert the truth."

100. "Where there is justice and righteousness, love rains in all seasons. Justice is a light to the nation; injustice poisons the soul of its people."

101. "Politics anchors on five indelibles: Prosperity for all, and order and peace as atmospheres, while righteousness and justice render them durables."[8]

---

[8] From Charles Mwewa, *A Case for Africa?s Liberty: The Synergistic Transformation of Africa and the West into First-World Partnerships* (Ottawa: ACP, 2021)

6 | FRIENDSHIP

1. "In the end, it will not be the people who praised you or fluttered you whom you will consider true friends; it will be those who warned you and redirected you when you were going in the wrong directions."

2. "A true friend criticizes you to your face in private but praises you openly in public."

3. "A friend to be a friend, must first be your confidante."

4. "A friend loves at all times."[9]

5. "It was never a true friendship if it ended because of irreconcilable differences."

6. "The value of true friendship is in having another human being care for,

---
[9] Proverbs 17:17

and treasure, you as they do for themselves."

7. "True friendship is not like chewing gum; you don't throw it out because the sweetness ended."

8. "A true friend is one who still believes in you when the world doubts you or rejects you. He/she is not a blind follower, but a true friend. He/she suffers your pain of rejection and even loses favor because they still believe in you."

9. *"Thirteen Friendship Traits*:

    a. At least one of them is of opposite sex/gender to yours - to gain the other perspectives;
    b. At least one of them is NOT your race, tribe or caste - to balance your filial approach;
    c. One should be a politician - to have easy access to services;

d. One of them should be in or knows, law - to navigate complex legal problems;
e. One of them should be religious - to keep your spiritual temperature at "normal" and to pray for you in difficulty times;
f. One of them should be poor or average; to remind you that you have a social responsibility here on earth;
g. One of them should be rich or a businessperson - to teach you that money is essential to progress;
h. One of them should be an accountant - to protect you and your money from investigators;
i. One of them should be a sinner - to keep you in constant prayer and spirit of evangelism;
j. One of them should be critical - to protect you from going astray and being puffed-up;
k. One of them should be a "Yes-yes-guy," to encourage you that your point of view matters;
l. One of them should not be your age mate - to keep you young and wise; and

m. One of them should be your lover - to make your life meaningful, long and purposeful."

10. *"11 True Friend Qualities*: 1. *Takes a Bullet for You* – true friends are willing to live and die for each other;
2. *Loves You, Not Yours* – true friends don't love each other because of what they will gain, but because of who they are;
3. *Communicates Regularly* – it is very hard to believe that you can be true friends and don't communicate often; true friends check on each other frequently;
4. *Not in It for Themselves* – true friends are not in it for themselves, but for the other;
5. *Creates Value* – if they are true friends, they will improve each other, and not devalue one another. If one friend only benefits, it's called a "Parasitic Friendship";
6. *Empathizes* - true friends identify with you, they aren't going to betray you;
7. *Specializes in Whole, Not in Parts* – true friends don't simply like you because of, they, rather, like you in spite of. They

endear the whole person – with all your foibles and your elegance as well;

8. *Defends* – true friends don't sell off one another, they defend each other;

9. *Increases You, Reduces Themselves* – that is expensive. If you find a friend who is willing to make you larger than them, you have a true friend;

10. *Cares for Your Heart and Soul* – very important – you're as important as your heart, and they who care for, and love you heartily, truly love you and are your true friends. They will remain with you come rain or sunshine. They will take care of you when everyone else leaves you. They will embrace you even and up to your grave; and

11. *Prays for You* – one of the greatest proofs that they are your true friends, is that they mention you before the Creator of Life."

11. "A friend is like a river of hope, everywhere it flows, plants of benevolence spring."

12. "True friendship doesn't wither with the sun of separation; it always flourishes in the shed of remembrances."

13. "A man's friend is his greatest and priceless treasure."

14. "A good friend dies for you a thousand times; an acquaintance turns against you when the going gets tough, but your enemy plots your downfall while he constantly smiles in your face."

15. "A man's wife and a woman's husband must be their truest and best friend, for there is no companionship too deep to be deprived of the true meaning of care, love, laughter, sorrow, and even tragedy other than the one experienced through marriage."

7 | VALUE OF PAIN

1. "The truth about pain is that it doesn't last forever; it is temporary. Most people fear to do the impossible because they fear pain. Everyone who has conquered pain, has defeated failure, disappointment, poverty and negative circumstances. The most precious gift on earth is human life, and every woman knows that it comes through pain. But women can also tell us that though painful, pain is temporary; it ends when the joy of life comes out. You can't move up or forward if you fear pain. Embrace pain, it is necessary to glory."

2. "If you are suffering persecution or hardships or if you are having problems and things seem not to be working your way or if you feel like you have no favor - don't fret, God is still on your side. Even those who fear, love and serve God go through troubles. But the good news is, you can trust Jesus Christ our Lord who also suffered and overcame."

3. "Fear to experience pain or the pleasure to evade it, are the two most motivating

factors for favorable action and behavior."

4. "The one who created comfort also created pain – so, there is a purpose for pain just as there is for comfort."

5. "The greatest the failure, the sweetest the victory; they who suffer long also deserve to have the jolliest feast."

8 | FAILURE GUARANTEE

1. "You're guaranteed to die poor, confused, embarrassed, disappointed and substanceless if this applies to you:

2. You have followed a leader who tells you that you are nothing without him;

3. You have followed a leader who is always becoming more powerful, richer and more famous when you are dwindling down - no name, no money, no property and no ideas;

4. You have followed a leader who shoots down your good intentions, he or she allows you not to advance in knowledge, not to compete with him or her, and etc.;

5. You have followed a man or woman who says that you have to follow his or her vision, and you can't have your own;

6. You have followed a leader who always wants the best, but hates you for wanting the same;

7. You are a leader who uses another leader's ideas and you have no clue what to do on your own;

8. You fear to leave a leader because he or she has told you you're nothing on your own;

9. You always give money, energy, ideas, praise and so on to a leader, but he or she gives you nothing in return, except requiring that you give him or her credit;

10. You think that your survival depends on another person's success or failure, stop right there;

11. You're afraid to offend people, you're afraid of what people will say, you're afraid to take initiative on your own – if this happens to you, rethink;

12. You keep procrastinating to start your own thing - days and years are going, but you are stagnated, always serving another like a slave."

9 | COVID-19

1. "Don't focus on the problem, but rather on a solution. The more we glorify Covid-19, the bigger than God it looks."

2. "The best way to prepare to defeat Covid-19, is to prepare to prevent infecting your neighbor."

3. "The cheapest method of ending Covid-19 pandemic is prevention, not curing."

4. "Fear is the strongest venom of Covid-19, if we can't fear, we can cure."

5. "During the Covid-19 pandemic, the more we are isolated, the more we should be united."

6. "The longer our social distance, the shorter our spiritual distance should get."

7. "One smart thing to do during Covid-19 pandemic is to love others as if they won't exist tomorrow, because it could be true."

8. "During the pandemic, blame less, accuse none and fight only one enemy, coronavirus."

9. "Covid-War is worse than First and Second World Wars combined, the enemy is invisible."

10. "The first reason you're staying at home during the pandemic, is to bond with your family."

11. "During the coronavirus war, everyone is a General if you command yourself to keep social distance."

12. "One lesson we all learn during the pandemic is that, money sometimes doesn't answer all questions."

13. "Crooks, fraudsters and the greedy, will still be carrying out their craft during the pandemic, know them."

14. "The golden rule of Covid-19 is, it is neither good to give nor to receive the virus."

15. "During the pandemic period, the best form of communication is non-verbal."

16. "If a government can't give its citizens food and water during the pandemic, remove it after the pandemic."

17. "Coronavirus is like a snow-ball, the more it rolls the bigger it spreads; stop it before it moves."

18. "Like a fire, if you don't prevent Covid-19 while it consumes your neighbor, you will be next."

19. "Don't neglect God's house during the Covid-19 pandemic, share your savings with His servants."

20. "Trump tried to put his own people in Covid-19 pathway in order to try and win an election."

21. "Covid-19 will disappear, if responsible behavior appears."

22. "Both delta and micron are lethal; the former kills in quality, the later in quantity."

23. "First, there was, 'Get vaccinated,' then, 'Get a second dose,' and then, 'Get a booster shot,' and again, 'Get a fourth dose,' will there be, 'Don't get vaccinated at all'?"

24. "Covid-19 moves as people move."

25. "Covid-19 is a multi-headed monster; you terminate one lethal head and other one more fatal reappears on its cadaver."

10 | BINARY QUANTUM

1. "To reach the highest heaven, you must endure the harshest hell;

2. To secure the lasting peace, you must fight and win the deadliest war;

3. To obtain to the highest faith, you must conquer the ugliest fear;

4. If you are willing to die, then you deserve to live;

5. If you can make the ultimate sacrifice, then you can obtain the purest trophy;

6. Being average is the recipe only failures treasure;

7. Those who have not been conquered, ignore the value of victory;

8. If you are not willing to go all the way to the finish, don't prepare for the journey;

9. Sweetness resides closest to bitterness [consider the proximity of anus to genitalia];

10. Pain and gain are two sides of the same coin; if you avoid pain, you disdain gain;

11. Rebounding from the steepest failure, gives way to the highest success;

12. To lead your people to prosperity, you must serve them from poverty.

13. To marry the right person, you should be the right person yourself.

14. If you want to continue feeding, you must stop and bury your seed;

15. If you want to be first, you should be last;

16. If you desire to be a leader, be a servant first;

17. When you are weak, then you are strong;

18. So, if you think you are standing firm, be careful that you don't fall" (1 Corinthians 10:12, Bible); and

19. If you miss childhood, grow awhile, and you will regain it in adulthood."

20. "Don't seek things that are easy, rather, let things become easy because you made them look so."

21. "If you want to be served, you should seek to serve first."

22. "History has shown that generations of those who oppressed others in time past, only bequeathed to their progeny a future filled with regrets and apologies."

23. "A seed must die in order to grow into a forest and sometimes it is better to sacrifice pleasure for a moment than to consummate it each time an opportunity presents itself; those who know how to control themselves, also know how to control others."

24. "The law of happiness is the mastery of pleasure and displeasure – those who do things in moderation will, in the final analysis, be happier than those who trade in extremes."

25. "There is no law against grace; those who give without expecting to be given back and those who lead without expecting bribes, will be treasured the most by and in history."

11 | RULE OF POWER

1. "In every age, epoch or era, power belongs to those who make rules. In every society, nation, club, activity or organization, those who fashion the law also control everyone. Whoever you give the power to make the rules for you, you also give them the license to govern your behavior, morality, value system, how far you can rise or fall, where and how you will live, and sometimes, if you live or die. That is why, like it or not, kings (and queens) and politicians will always rule."

2. "The rule of bad laws is tyranny."

3. "If tyranny becomes law, organized revolt becomes the means to restore order."

4. "Those who make rules will have power."

5. "Temper power with grace, as judgment is tempered with mercy."

6. "To sustain justice, those who investigate must be investigated; and those who judge, should be judged."

7. "Power does not corrupt, only the abuse of it does."

8. "Power without principles is like children mishandling Trinitrotoluene (TNT)."

9. "The rule of power without rules, first ruins the handler, and then the handled."

10. "Even if the constitution grants you all the power, in governing, restraint is the charm that opens the favor chalice."

11. "Mandate is the key, law is the guide, justice is the flame, power is the vehicle, and delivery is the destination within the labyrinth called government."

12. "I want to get in power. I want to get in power so that I can change those things I cannot without power. I want to get in power after I have made money elsewhere, so that I don't use power as a means to enriching myself. I want to get in power badly, because through power, I can create legislation that can empower people to live their lives with dignity,

without poverty and with hope. That is why I want to get in power."

13. "Power and money have one thing in common: The more power or money one has, the slowly but steadily blinded they get. In their world of overwhelmed glory, they see no empathy, respect no virtue and tolerate no weakness. They see everyone and everything as tools of their pleasure and even of their self-improvement. Those who helped them to succeed are forgotten and divergent voices are silenced. Only those who flatter them or offer them self-aggrandized glory are embraced. In the end, their blindness become their liabilities and down they fall."

14. "Restraint is the greatest companion to wise leadership. When those less powerful than you challenge you or your position, the natural reaction is to silence them or worse. This is unwise. The best thing to do when challenged or questioned by those less powerful or lower in ranks than you are, is to stop, listen attentively, process deeply, and

even if your faculties cry for retaliation, contain yourself and respond with grace. If and when possible, give your response another time – when you have all internal configurations in check."

15. "The best model of treating your subordinates is the *Child Model*; you treat them with patience and discipline them with love."

12 | GOVERNMENT & LEADERSHIP

1. "Wherever humans shall gather, and there choose, by default or election, a leader, such a woman or man should ascribe, first and foremost, to divine law, as unimpeachable authority and foundation for morality and policy, and then thereby the governed shall demand to, supplemented only by sound and congenial human law, be led by such men and women so confirmed."

2. "For governance, effective leadership is not a luxury; it is a rare commodity, a currency. It consists in shooting directly at the demons of corruption, lethargy and lack of innovation, while at the same time remaining vigilant not to be stained by them."

3. "A nation must be governed, in the least, by good laws; otherwise by men and women of integrity."

4. "All governments, bad or good, are recognized by God; but only good governments have God's blessings."

5. "Nations are like humans; if they treat the poor within them well, they will hoard good future fortunes."

6. "No man receives any position except it was given him by God. It is not how big but how dedicated we're to our task that matters. God will not reward us based on quantity but quality of our work. So, never envy another person's work, do yours well and give it the very best, however insignificant it may seem."

7. "Any government, no matter where on earth, has no right to spend the taxpayers' money on officials' pleasures and leisure, unless doing so is a consequence of the latter's demonstration of hard work."

8. "All governments, bad or good, are recognized by God; but only good governments have God's blessings."

9. "A government is like a home, only at a large scale. Like a home, it should do or act in its citizens' best interest even if that puts its own worldview at loggerheads."

10. "Anyone who qualifies should run for government office. If a government is not accounting for all it receives in revenues, it must be removed and its officials prosecuted. Government is not a means for personal aggrandizement; it's a privileged responsibility."

11. "Government should not pay its citizens for doing nothing, but government must pay anyone who does something."

12. "If in a country a few make use of the majority of that country's revenues, government has failed."

13. "If in a country there are poor people, government has work to do."

14. "You don't need a Christian leader or a Christian Cabinet, though that may be a bonus, but a godly people to humble themselves, pray and turn from their wicked ways, to exalt a nation."

15. "It's a travesty that we talk of the glorious past as days of responsibility and prosperity, but forget that those days were, relatively, governed by men informed of high ethical standards."

16. "Christopher Columbus didn't discover the new world by a map or a stroke of intellectual genius, but with faith and the guidance of the Word. The world cannot be governed by intellect and knowledge alone, but by every wisdom that comes from the heart of God."

17. *"On delegation:* Every leader of people must learn the art of delegation. There are three types of delegation: (1) Nominal delegation: A leader must delegate as a means of grooming the next set of leaders. Because no-one can learn leadership in a classroom, people will become great leaders if they can (a) observe a great leader, or (b) lead-by-doing. So this type of delegation is essential to continuity of the vision; (2) Crisis delegation: A leader must delegate because a situation has arisen that demands his temporary absence from current leadership obligations; and (3) Emergency delegation: A leader must delegate because a crisis has turned into a permanent emergence, e.g. a leader cannot be present due to a prolonged illness, disciplinary action, resignation, termination or death. In whichever type, a leader should be looking for a person (not people in general) who should assume the responsibility. This individual must know they are on stand-by, must be trained to lead before a crisis or an emergency arises, and the leader should

be consistent in delegating through this individual (changing people for delegation may be politically correct, but is a poor mode of delegation. It is usually done by insecure leaders. It creates half-baked leaders; it induces jealousies and competitions and breeds controversy in the demise of the leader). Seamless succession is a mark of true leadership acumen."

18. *"On leadership arsenal:* A leader must have the knowledge to understand the competing options; the wisdom to make right and informed decisions; the courage to dispel criticisms; the flexibility to change; the faith to try new things; the grace to manage pressure; and the confidence to lead."

19. *"On problem-solving:* A true leader identifies problems in order to solve them. And in solving them, a true leader separates people from the problem in order to fashion solution to the problem. Non-leaders identify problems and blame them on the people, because non-leaders think of the people as a problem."

QUOT-EBOS

20. *"On teamwork:* 'Ants don't have leaders, but they store up food during harvest season.' In a typical colony of ants, there could be millions of nests divided into queen ants, worker ants and warrior ants. The central role of the queen ant is reproduction, not leadership. Ants survive by teamwork – they find food, store food, and invade other nests and fight – all by teamwork. Great leaders always move their organizations towards leaderless systems – a stage where the people have grown to know the system too well and they can literally govern themselves by teamwork. The more people need a leader, the far away the leader is from being a true leader, and the far away those people are from reaching their greatest potential."

21. *"On purpose:* In leadership, the purpose of the goal is more important than the size of it."

22. *"On ownership of success and failure:* A leader may not be an expert in everything, but they must know what is going on in every department of the organization or obligation. Afterall, a leader owns both the successes and failures of their organization or obligation."

23. *"On leadership dynamics:* Leading people in an organization or nation is pretty much like leading sheep and goats. Unlike goats which are exploratory, interactive, engaging and investigative in nature, sheep are more laid back and sometimes just plain 'sheepish.' Goats are naturally curious and independent. But they can tend to get into more trouble than sheep, too. Sheep have very strong flocking instinct, and become agitated when separated from their posse. Sheep have an overall better resistance to pasture parasites because they have evolved eating close to the ground. But this puts them in close contact with roundworms, tapeworms, and etc. Goats, in comparison, eat off the ground and have less contact with parasites on the ground. But goats have a less developed

natural ability to resist parasitic infections. The simple fact is that both sheep and goats have issues and leading them involves employing varying styles. Here are four: (1) Some humans are like sheep, calm and collected but 'sheepish' and vulnerable to risks. (2) Some humans are like goats, engaging, outgoing and intelligent, but vulnerable to dangers. (3) Generally, for sheep-like obligation, lead from the front with care, knowledge and understanding. For goat-like obligations, lead from behind but still with care, knowledge and understanding. (4) For both sheep-like and goat-like behaviors, there are four responsibilities you have as a leader: (a) feeding them; (b) teaching them; (c) restoring or discipline them; (d) protecting them."

24. *"On category of followers:* In any leadership arrangement, the people are divided into four categories of followers: Sheep; goats; cattle/bulls; and horses. With sheep, the leader leads from the front – trailblazing and guiding the way through example and care. With cattle or bulls,

the leader leads from the back – because going in front jeopardizes the leader's own wellbeing. He may be trampled upon and killed. With horses, the leader mounts them and leads from the vertical – because the leader and the horse are of similar strength and wit. Some people are exactly like sheep (good mannered, easy to guide and direct and generally weak-willed individuals) these the leader must recognize and lead from the front; they will never stub them in the back. Goat-like followers are savvy, subtle, agile, flexible but vulnerable and left to themselves, they can be self-destructed and destructive. These lead from the back because you need to see where they are going and guide and direct appropriately. These will not deliberately stub the leader in the back although they may be a danger to themselves. And they may deserve a weep of discipline from time to time. Cattle or bulls are strong and usually self-willed. They cannot be led from the front or they will trample over the leader and kill his vision. They can be very critical but they genuinely have the power to destroy the leader. So, you lead them from the back and sides – constantly monitoring their movements and activities because they can be very, very dangerous and destructive if left to themselves. Like goats, they deserve a weep of discipline from time to time. Finally, horses – these are strong, intelligent but very trusted, obedient, tamable and dependable. Such kind of followers you lead vertically because they are equal to the leader in every respect. They need vertical guidance and measured discipline in order to keep them focused and effective. Horse followers can break new grounds and win battles together with the leader. Over 90 percent of human behavior is sheep-like."

25. *"On ultimate goal of leadership:* A leader is a teacher, first and foremost. In sports they may be called a coach or instructor or trainer; in education, a professor or instructor; in military, a general or commander; in the home, a parent; in the church, a pastor or elder or deacon; in politics, a mayor or premier or governor or prime minister or president or king or queen; in martial arts, a master

or instructor; and etc. A teacher's ultimate aim is to get students become teachers, so a leader's ultimate aim is not to make followers, but to lead followers into becoming leaders."

26. "Dedicated leaders are the world's most endangered species."

27. "When you discriminate and draw boundaries of apartheid, racism, bigotry, prejudice, intolerance, bias, or chauvinism, you become narrow-minded and incapable of being a true human leader."

28. "In life it is not about what happens so much as in how you respond to what happens that matters. Success is not linear, and neither is influence."

29. "Love is the highest characteristic of human leadership."

30. "Ten characterisitcs of caring leadership: (1) Caring Leaders are Servants; (2) Caring Leaders Earn Respect; (3) They Bring Higher Social Returns; (4) Caring Leaders are People-Oriented; (5) Caring Leaders are Invisible; (6) Caring Leaders Touch the Core of Man; (7) Caring Leaders Leave Lasting Legacies; (8) Caring Leaders are Trailblazers; (9) Caring Leaders are Change-Oriented; and (10) Caring Leaders are Disciplined."

31. "Knowing how to deal with adversity is one of the most decorated symbols of leadership."

32. "Leadership is the exertion of influence on people's attitudes in order to bring the best out of them."

33. "Through contribution, we leave marks that will inspire others to see the light in the dark of life's nights."

34. "Show me a real champion, a real life winner and I will show you a man that leads by example and shows others how to win."

35. "Government should only be sought if the glory of the people is your goal, their happiness, your dream, and the suffering of which they may be prone to, becomes yours."

13 | MONEY & WELLBEING

1. "Money is good; Money answers all things; Money is essential to life; Money is a god of freedom; and money does not discriminate."

2. "Money is not evil; Money is not the root of evil; Money is not the root of all evil; and only lust and greed with money is the root of evil or all evil."

3. "You can get money by working for it; planning for it; investing for profit; for money makes money."

4. "Money is everywhere; even where you are."

5. "Money is in poor as well as rich nations."

6. "Everyone who wants to be rich must not think farther than their own locale. Everything is there around you to become rich."

7. "Money is everywhere you look; your job is to figure out how to access it legally."

8. "Money is attractively weak; it can be lured with a right bait."

9. "What explains why some people are richer than others is the presence of money with one, and the absence of it with another. Poor people have little or no money at all. And it seems like in every society the people who have a lot of money also have more power and influence."

10. "Money is single most distinguishing mark between those who struggle and those who enjoy plenty. Money is the most common name and the most used item on the globe. With it problems seem to disappear, and without it, despair rages. Whether people know it or not, love it or hate it, money answers almost all things."

11. "Despite the fact that money is that common, most people either lack it or if they have it, don't know how to keep it. People do everything to make money, and yet lack the skill to keep it. Every day people are going to school, college and universities in order to increase the acquisition of money. Every day people are going to work to earn money. And yet, the very thing that people so struggle to make, eludes them and brings them so many anxieties."

12. "In every society, people understand that achievement is proportional to how much money one makes. It does not matter how you define achievement, if there is no money to show for it, no-one will believe that you have achieved much. You may acquire trophies, win medals, and accrue memorabilia or a good name, but if there is no money accompanying, all such accolades, people will doubt your achievement."

13. "The journey of one mile begins with a step. Similarly, the journey towards one million dollars begins with a penny."

14. "When you get to your department store or to your local convenience store to purchase some groceries, you will probably notice how prices are fixed. They all seem to be one cent less. Instead of $5, it will be $4.99 or $19.95 for $20. Why is it so? Apart from the psychological impact that it has on your price perception, it simply means that every cent matters. If you have one cent less, you may not be able to get what you want or need."

15. "Until your attitude towards money changes, you cannot be rich."

16. "The difference between successful business-people and struggling ones is profit. Profit is the difference between costs and revenue. The rich make more profit on their principal than the poor.

Poor people are either making losses or nothing at all. To be a rich person you must be making profit in one way or the other. You cannot do anything for nothing. You must always profit from your venture."

17. "Profit leads to happiness."

18. "Many people are ashamed to be seen to be profit-motivated. If you are not profit-motivated, you are both standing still and not going anywhere or you are dying and going backwards."

19. "You can only benefit from the investments you make. Your best investments are those you have not yet made."

20. "Money and sex have one thing in common - most households use it, but few take time to improve it."

21. "There are four leadership principles about money. First, those who have money rule over those who do not have it. Second, success or achievement is tied to money, no matter how one defines success. Third, money gives authority. And fourth, money is power."

22. "Money and Satan have one thing in common; they both desire to control you."

23. "For everything there is a will to purchase, God has given the power to find the money."

24. "'Money, come to me; serve me; work for me; be easily found; and don't leave me': that's a declaration every believer must make."

25. "If you despise money, it will despise you, too."

26. "If you believe that money is hard to come by it will always be hard for you to find it."

27. "I know anyone can make money, if they put their mind to making it."

28. "I know money is conquerable - because most people who want to use it, don't spend time knowing how to make it."

29. "I know money obeys - because if you call its name, it responds."

30. "*Ceteris paribas*, one grain of corn has the profitable potential to bring a bumper harvest – but only if it's cultivated."

31. "I know money is easy to make - because it is in circulation."

32. "I know money is easy to find - because it is usually in every man's wallet and in every woman's purse."

33. "I know money is a god - because if you keep it, it eludes you; if you use it, it gains more."

34. "Spend your life learning a business, and not a career, unless your career will be a business. Most rich people are in business."

35. "Jesus was right, there will always be the poor among us - you can put financial info in front of them, they will not find it."

36. "I've observed that only about 10 percent take time to understand complex ideas, such as money - majority love to 'like' easy things."

37. "If you spend most of your time on social media and still make no money, stop, spend more time where you will make money."

38. "If your financial model only makes money for you once every month, you have a wrong model; strive to make money every day."

39. "If begging is in your long-term financial planning goals, you are dead-on-arrival at your destination."

40. "Most people know it but ignore it to their detriment: There's more blessings in giving than in receiving; go ahead and give, don't just beg or ask."

41. "Profit is defined as the art of making additional money."

42. "In every society, people understand that achievement is proportional to how much money one makes."

43. "Money is like fish; it is everywhere in the waters. He who uses the right instrument will catch a lot of it."

44. "The journey to wealth begins with a penny, so every child has the potential to become rich."

45. "Don't be in a hurry to count your dollars; count, rather, that your dollars have given another person a life."

46. "A rich man without peace is worse than a poor man with hope."

47. "If your riches cannot bring you happiness, and if your poverty makes you happy, it is a curse to be either!"

48. "Poverty is always bad; the poor may not."

49. "Riches are good, but the rich may not always be the wisest people on earth."

50. "Humans proportionally give less and help least when they have plenty of money."

51. "No matter how rich you are, you have only one mouth and only one stomach."

52. "A wise rich person will enjoy his riches more by giving it out to many poor people who will enjoy it with him."

53. "No matter how much you possess or how rich you are, you're only a steward for another, usually a lazy, foolish or sleazy relative or government."

54. "The poorest person on earth is the one with the money which they cannot enjoy."

55. "Only he who can buy everything with nothing is richer than all."

56. "While money answers all things, wisdom solves all problems."

57. "If you can make money for another person, you can make money for yourself, too; the wisdom is, can you start earlier before someone else erodes your métier?"

58. "It's that simple: If you can make money for someone else, you can make money for yourself, too."

59. "The poor have less or no sources of money; the wealth make money from multiple sources."

60. "Money promises the world, and it can deliver."

61. "Look for money wherever it may be found; hold it tight though it may be slippery."

62. "If a man, health and of sound mind, lacks the means to provide for and protect those he loves, he is worth more dead than alive."

63. "Money in another person's account, pockets, purse or wallet can easily be yours."

14 | PERCEPTION

1. "Perception is like a duck; calm on the surface but paddling underneath."

2. "People look at the outward appearance."

3. "Perception is giving people a positive impression of you. It is different from deception."

4. "As a leader, you are attracting people every day by the way you appear. It is your responsibility to know how you want people to perceive you. In leadership, perception is not a lifestyle, it is a strategy. You use it to achieve certain ends. Every great leader, in history as well as now, has used the power of perception to advance their own ends. Without perception, people will not sacrifice, give gifts or give themselves to causes. Nations, great and small, invest enormously in the way they are perceived. What we call diplomacy is nothing but a perception front."

5. "If you've reached the end of your wit; you are shaken to the core; you don't know what to do; you are pressed by the worries of life; you are at your end;

you've reached the lowest. Know this, the lowest you reach, the most blessed you're. Why, because at your deepest bottom, you can only look up - nothing else helps. And when you look up, guess what, the arms of Jesus will be widely open to hear you, fish you out, sustain you, provide for you, save you, and bring you out in victorious triumph. I have been amazed how that when I am weak, then I am strong."

6. "How things look may not be how things are; only those who perceive can tell the difference."

7. "Leadership is perception."

8. "If you perceive that your tomorrow is fine, your today will proceed very well."

15 | MOTIVATION

1. "Most people who do much in life and change things have learned to "refuse." They refuse to give up; to be belittled, to be boxed into circles, to be stripped of purpose, to be cheated on their vision, to have their dreams die, to be used by others, to be defined by their limitations, to be confined to what they have, to be told what to do, to be shaped by their environment, to be forced to quit, to be called "losers', to be shamed by past failures, to be deterred by rejection, to be trodden under by the devil, to be framed by their history, and to be told, 'You're not important.'"

2. "'Consider it pure joy, my brothers and sisters, whenever you face trials of many kinds.'[10] Therefore, do not run away from trouble, run towards trouble; do not fear to face or embrace trouble, thrive in trouble; do not pray for trouble to end, ask God for more grace during trouble. The more the trouble, the greatest the joy - because nothing, absolutely nothing, can separate you from the love of God which is in Christ Jesus, your Lord."

---

[10] James 1:2

3. "A mistake can be the greatest teacher when you look for the seed of good in it."

4. "Sorrow may endure for the night, but joy comes in the morning," (Psalm 30:5, Bible).

5. "If the farmer plants choice and healthy seeds, he will be guaranteed of a good harvest."

6. "Seasons teach us two lessons about success: Preparation and opportunity."

7. "Caring is the basis for humanity and the flame that keeps human life alive."

8. "And David was greatly distressed; for the people spake of stoning him, because the soul of all the people was grieved, every man for his sons and for his daughters: but David encouraged himself in the LORD his God."[11]

---

[11] 1 Samuel 30:6

QUOT-EBOS

9. "You can forget an ugly past by beginning to create a beautiful one today."

10. "Live smart - speak well; make money; Attract others; do right; and do more in little time."

11. "Bees need flowers to make honey. Beauty attracts sweetness. Use what is 'beautiful' about you to attract what is 'sweet.'"

12. "Stop being a coward. The definition of a coward is one who gives up when the going gets tough."

13. "Let nobody intimidate you; let nobody abuse you; let nobody cheat you; let nobody make you their slave."

14. "Be like a horse, it prides in facing danger head on."

15. "Many things are not in black and white; but all become clearer the more you focus."

16. "God is happy with those who pray; but even happier with those who pray and do."

17. "Right and good are desirable qualities; but if you may, be right - sometimes good is the enemy of right."

18. "If you stay in the right lane, you can reach your destination."

19. "Roses have thorns, honey has bees, and success has enemies."

20. "Think big, reason wide, search more, start again, dream long, and encourage yourself."

21. "You're just as good as a millionaire next door, only take time to think of an idea."

22. "Don't put your trust in a man - it's just a matter of time you will be disappointed. Rather, trust God, believe in yourself."

23. "Please, please, don't give up; hold on tight to your vision, dream, plan, life. Quitters are losers."

QUOT-EBOS

24. "Cheer up, everyone who did something great suffered great persecution."

25. "Always walk with your head high, your feet one step ahead, and your voice eloquent enough to be heard."

26. "Let no one despise these: Your youth, business plans, success strategy, investments, efforts, or your dream."

27. "Nothing seems to be going well for you; well, it seems you are almost breaking through; it's darkest before it's bright."

28. "Stop wasting time waiting for the right time; the right time is now - to become what you've always wanted to be."

29. "No witch, no demon, not even Satan has power over you; you win even before you fight. That's who you're in Christ."

30. "Don't fear the future, only fear God. Those who plan your grave, will be erecting your triumph."

31. "If you have failed recently or in the past, that's still good news - because you aren't failing again. Your destiny calls."

32. "See yourself holding millions of moneys, and you will."

33. "If you've been told that you're a loser, ugly or anything that bad, ignore; know that you're a winner, beautiful and excellent."

34. "Believe that the future belongs to you, yes it does. No disease or accident will take you before your time."

35. "Don't allow anything or anyone to write you off; you should live like a champion and die like a victor."

36. "The evilest character in entire world history (Satan) can enjoy pleasure; surely, God will also give you many things to enjoy."

37. "Those terms like victory, favor, blessings, success, good health, or promotion can now be yours - simply believe and step out."

QUOT-EBOS

38. "You have suffered much, now claim your portion and reject to give in to the enemy."

39. "You ultimately become what you think, attract what you feel, create what you imagine, possess what you believe, and change what you despise."

40. "When I was a child, I saw and believed only what was before me; now that I am an adult, I see and unbelieve in a world full of possibilities."

41. "If you keep falling when you should be rising, your energy level is too low."

42. "If you take care of the things that matter to God; God will take care of the things that matter to you."

43. "Give more energy, strength and time to those things that will be alive when you are dead, than to those things that will perish when you die."

44. "Remember to remember when you are alive the people who will remember you when you are dead."

45. "Encouragement is the only potent drug the overdose of which has only positive effects."

46. "If your present world seems to come to an end, create a new world."

47. "Where possible, ask God, he can be your unbeatable motivation."

16 | AFRICA & AMERICA

1. "If Africa and America were thieves, Africa would be a petty thief who steals from his own people; America a robber who steals from others."

2. "Africa is the world's next frontier – in the West the road is ended; in Africa, it's just trended."

3. "America owes Africa in human terms, in economic fortune, in labor count, and in future survival."

4. "I have lived half my life in Africa and half in the West. My observation: Africans can do anything Westerners can do; Africans can think just as creative as Westerners can."

5. "Africa and the West try so much to be opposites - until you learn that one sits on resources it's lazy to develop and the other feeds on that laziness."

6. "Africa – oh how I love and hate you at the same time – recently I dedicated a book to your beauty and you didn't read it. Another told you what was written in it, that I had insulted you, and you told people not to read my book. In Africa, it

is possible to live in poverty all your life when all the time your land was laden with gold and diamonds. I want to change that."

7. "When the road comes to an end in America, they extend it by the way of Africa."

8. "The cradle is more important than the building; those who despise Africa now must know that their support rests in Africa."

9. "Africa has no other way to go, but up."

10. "American ingenuity and future depend on aligning its interests with Africa's; when this is absent, the former fades, the later survives."

17 | VALUE OF THE PAST

1. "God gives us an opportunity to review the past, to own the present and envision the future. Everything that happened to us and what we did or said in the past is a wealth of valuable lessons (no matter how bitter and painful they were). The present is a welcome challenge – because it enables us to live out what we planned in the past and it gives us a chance not to repeat an atrocious past. But the future is a blank cheque – we can write a new story or design a new plan or believe that the best is yet to come. Of the past, present and the future, the only one we have power over is the present – therefore it is a waste of life to waste the present."

2. "In the *Bank of Past Glory*, you can presently debit any amount for future spending."

3. "Future triumphs are often born from past mistakes."

4. "Don't forget where you came from; you may need it to know where you are going."

5. "The past is necessary if there is to be a future."

6. "Where there is no time, there is no past."

7. "Without the past, there will be no memories."

8. "It takes less effort to reconstruct the past than to imagine the future."

9. "The past is more mature than the present and future combined; we all have spent more time in the past, less in the present, and none in the future."

10. "The past is the best teacher, the present is the best parent, and the future is the best child."

18 | TRUST

1. "Ignorantly or knowingly, people disobey a fundamental precept in the Bible: Do not put trust in any man or woman. There is nowhere in the Bible it says a man or woman should put trust in another man or woman. We can trust others, but not to put trust in another man, there is a difference. A person who trusts another person is like a warrior without a shield;[12] will be disappointed;[13] is cursed;[14] will be deceived;[15] is a fool;[16] is hopeless;[17] is lost;[18] it is impossible to trust man;[19] will go astray;[20] is helpless;[21] is a bad idea;[22] will be polluted;[23] will never know what hit them;[24] is not worthy of trust;[25] will be weakened;[26] is limited;[27] people will not be there when you need them most;[28]

---

[12] Psalm 118:8
[13] Micah 7:5-8
[14] Jeremiah 17:5-6
[15] Jeremiah 9:4
[16] Proverbs 28:26
[17] Isaiah 2:22
[18] Psalm 146:3
[19] John 2:24-25
[20] Psalm 40:3-4
[21] Psalm 118:9-13
[22] Psalm 118:9
[23] Proverbs 25:26
[24] Hebrews 4:12
[25] Colossians 3:23
[26] Philippians 4:13
[27] Matthew 10:28
[28] Psalm 46:1

man's justice is unjust;[29] man by nature is vengeful;[30] trusting in another man or woman is idolatry."[31]

2. "Value the opinion of another; respect all human beings; but trust only God."

3. "Anything that takes in oxygen and releases carbon-dioxide cannot be trusted; least anything that does neither."

4. "Trust is like a symphony orchestra; keep every instrument and voice in tune."

5. "When trust is lost, look everywhere to find it."

---

[29] Romans 12:19
[30] Romans 13:4
[31] Exodus 20:1-26

19 | MASTERPIECE

1. "Inside all of us is a masterpiece. A masterpiece is an artist's or craftsman's best piece of work. A masterpiece has three essential qualities: It is rare, and of rare quality; it is transcendental, that is, it is inspirational, eternal and sublime; and it is the best or new in its class. Created humans are the Creator's masterpiece. When the Creator looks at us, he sees his best work. There is no junk or useless human-being; all are valuable, a masterpiece."

2. "So, my friend, excel, exude beauty, sophistication and excellence. Do you have a talent, excel in it. Do you have ability, exercise it. Do you have a dream, fulfil it? Do you have opportunities, use them. Just don't procrastinate; step out in faith – stand out and be counted…because you're a masterpiece."

3. "Did you know that winter, spring, summer and fall are consistent with snow, water, fire or light and air or wind; and to bitterness, sourness, sweetness and saltiness? Balance these, succeed in life."

4. "Time and patience create a masterpiece."

5. "Life is like a piece of pottery; it takes time and creativity to create but only milliseconds and a little stupidity to destroy."

6. "When a masterpiece is missing, the entire enterprise collapses; that part of you that you can't live without, is your masterpiece."

7. "A man's gift makes room for him and brings him before the great [and] when a man's ways please the LORD, he makes even his enemies to be at peace with him," (Proverbs 18:16; 16:7, Bible).

20 | THE STONE OF GOLD

1. "Gold is *the* Stone. Unlike other stones, gold is precious and treasurable. What makes a stone like gold both costly and valuable is that (1) it is rare – not found everywhere like dirt is; (2) it passes through very high temperatures to make it pure, shiny and clean; and (3) it is hardened to make it durable. Anyone can turn from being a common person (common dirt) to become a valuable person (gold) when they set themselves apart as special and of value (because they are); when they allow difficulties not to break them down, but to refine them in good character and resolve; and when they are hardened against those who entice them not to be of self-restraint and decisive."

2. "Inside of every child is gold, unpolished; its impurities can only come out by measured and reasonable discipline, which may also include a gentle spanking."

3. "Each small hit you make, gets you nearest to gold."

4. "I want gold for Christmas. I want a big piece of gold for holding. I want many ounces of gold so that I can have plenty of money. I want to find the stone that is very expensive. I don't want a stone that is cheap and is thrown away. If I have a great piece of gold, I can buy a house; I can buy a golf course and I can give more money to the poor. I truly want lot and lots of gold."

5. "Gold is just a piece of stone until it is passed through intense heat and it receives a great beating, then it becomes precious and expensive. So, is human life."

21 | POWER

1. In "The Lord's Prayer", Jesus protects us from absolute power politics. When He says pray that, "For Thine is the kingdom and the power and the glory forever," He restricts us to what extent we can give man and God the power. Power in the hands of man must be with restraints of checks and balances – because man with absolute power becomes corrupt. But Jesus says that absolute power in the hands of God is safe. Ever wondered that despite all the power that God has, He neither abuses it nor uses it against us? Man would easily do that.

2. Adam and Eve sinned when they were (a) perfect and (b) in paradise. I used to think that people sin because they are not perfect and because they live in an imperfect world. But now I realize that people can sin even when they are perfect and live in a perfect world, just like perfect Adam and perfect Eve did. It seems that not sinning is a choice, not a condition.

3. King David as a man did so many bad things: He committed adultery, lied, murdered, and etc., and yet when Paul recounts the history of Israel, he says that God called David, "A man after God's own heart." Have you pondered on the fact that David as a *man* was not very perfect, although as a *child* he could have been? And still God found him, as a "man," not as a child, to be His *man*. You may have sinned,

done horrible things against God, even after you have known Him, but if your heart is right before God, even after terrible sins, you can still be God's man. After-all, it seems, God values a repentant heart, not a perfect, sinless heart.

22 | INSPIRATION

1. "Satan likes people who read about prayer; loves people who hate prayer; hates people who know the power of prayer; but only fears the people who pray."

2. "Prayer is not a noun; it is a verb, an action word, so start praying right now."

3. "Every parent has a responsibility to pray for their family, daily, if possible."

4. "Teach people how to pray for others, they will automatically learn how to pray for themselves."

5. "Prayer is like an exercise (or a gym) - everyone knows it is good, but very few find time to do it."

6. "Three benefits of praying for others: (1) It is God's will; (2) It is an exercise of God's love; and (3) Because prayer is the assigned method whereby God meets the needs of others."

7. "Prayer and peace are like a person and their shadow; where one is the other follows."

8. "Intercession is a double-edged sword; you cannot pray for others without God also meeting your needs at the same time."

9. "Praying for other people shows that we love others even above self. It shows we love God and what He loves."

10. "Intercession is love in action; you cannot hate who you pray for."

11. "Do not be guilty that you did not pray with words, be concerned that you did not pray with your heart. The prayer that touches the heart of God, flows from the heart of man (people)."

12. "Prayer is designed to be in secret. I find the solace of my car the best and safest prayer closest ever. Use every secret space you have to offer a prayer. Pray often. But pray for others most often, and for those weak among peoples on a daily basis, if possible."

13. "Prayer saves the sick:[32] We know that prayer heals the sick, did we also know that prayer can save the sick and also have God forgive their sins? This is one of the greatest mysteries of prayer in grace; that when people are hopelessly

---

[32] James 5:15

sick, God's grace is abundantly available, and as you pray for the sick, God also saves them and ushers them into Heaven. Praying for the sick — especially those in coma and those who will not live — is the most urgent calling of every-day Christianity. Notice the verses in 5 translations: "And the prayer of faith shall save the sick, and the Lord shall raise him up; and if he has committed sins, they shall be forgiven him."[33] "...and the prayer of faith shall heal the sick, and the Lord shall raise him up; and if he be one who has committed sins, it shall be forgiven him."[34] "...and the prayer of faith will heal him who is sick, and the Lord will raise him up. If he has committed sins, he will be forgiven."[35] "...and the prayer of the faith shall save the distressed one, and the Lord shall raise him up, and if sins he may have committed, they shall be forgiven to him."[36] "And the prayer of faith shall save the sick, and the Lord shall raise him up; and if he has committed sins, they shall be forgiven him."[37]

---

[33] [King James Version]
[34] [Darby Bible Translation]
[35] [World English Bible]
[36] [Young's Literal Translation]
[37] [Geneva Study Bible]

14. "'For I know the plans that I have for you,' declares the LORD, 'plans for welfare and not for calamity to give you a future and a hope. Then you will call upon Me and come and pray to Me, and I will listen to you....'"[38] God declares He has a plan for all of us – a good and prosperous plan. Why should He ask us to call (pray) upon Him and He will listen if He has all planned for us? Precisely why we pray – to trigger God's plan for us into motion. This verse does say that God only knows the plans He has for us. It does not say that He is putting that plan into action. It is our responsibility to ask Him to put it into action. And the only way we do that is when we pray."

15. "Prayer is essential to the fight against temptations as watching is to the security of treasures."

16. "The posture of your prayer does not matter; what matters is the condition of your heart."

17. "When prayer intrudes into worry, worry is converted into peace."

18. "Prayer is the only key that opens doors locked from the inside."

---

[38] Jeremiah 29:11 and 12

19. "Prayer is the most gracious route of God meeting our needs, the most elevated position of honoring God, and the fastest method of arriving at the Throne of God."

20. "Prayer is not a weakness, a strength it is, but sometimes both, so that in praying we express our own dependence in God's secure providence, and in this way, we also access God's divine truth reserved for those whose hearts are contrite and broken."

21. "Jesus cannot do anything in the world except His people pray. Jesus said, "A branch cannot bear fruit without the vine." Ever wondered that the opposite is also true, "A vine bears fruit through its branches." So, without its branches, the vine cannot be fruitful. So, it is with Christ and His church (His people), if they don't pray, He cannot move. Oh, that we should pray, and not faint.

22. "We reap what we sow, not necessarily where we sow."

23. "Jesus is our advocate (lawyer; intercessor) before the Father.[39] An advocate speaks on behalf of the accused - he represents the accused before the court/judge. He represents them when they have done something wrong or criminal. He presents evidence or makes arguments on their behalf. Human advocates are limited to what they can prove because they depend on what the accused did and said. Jesus, on the other hand, can represent every person because the proof is himself; he was punished for the wrongs/sins/crimes of everyone he represents. He presents his own life and blood as evidence that punishment has already occurred and so people should be free/acquitted. The devil is the accuser of the brethren.[40] Whenever the devil wants to accuse/condemn you (and he has the right to do so because we are all sinners), Christ is always there at the right hand of the Father,[41] and Jesus stands up daily and defends you, because he bears the mark of the crucifixion in his hands. Therefore, because of the intercessions of Christ, we can all live in victory and die as if we never sinned."

---

[39] 1 John 2:1
[40] Revelation 12:10
[41] Acts 7:55-56; Romans 8:34; Ephesians 1:20; Colossians 3:1, Romans 8:34

24. "Prayer is good for the body - it brings balance to the system, which leads to peace that passes human understanding."

25. "Although you live in the world, your battles shall be won in the spirit, and only with two weapons - the name of Jesus Christ and the Word of God; there is no evidence anywhere, in heaven or on earth or in hell, that these weapons have ever failed, they only succeed."

26. "To tell someone that 'I will pray for you' is a prayer in itself, and usually God grants such requests."

27. "Prayer is communication and loving relationship with the Father, frequently engaged in for various reasons (needs, wants, praise, thanksgiving, petitions, supplications, requests, intercessions, worship and sometimes just simply talking or having fun with God) in the name of Jesus Christ."

28. "Prayer is the ladder we use if we want to access our heavenly investments."

29. "Not to pray is weakness, the first failure you fail yourself. When we first came into this world, we cried. and God answered."

30. "Prayer is a trade-off; it's trading off our needs for God's wants."

31. "When I pray, I am saying, 'God has trusted me with the earth, and I trust He will provide the resources.'"

32. "Prayer is smarter than intellectualism; the later requires the use of the mind, the former, the use of the heart."

33. "Prayer is smart-talk; words only doing what a thousand hands can't do."

34. "He who prays to God is wiser than he who votes in an election."

35. "I have heard it said that prayer is talking to God; and I can add that it is God's failure not to work for us."

36. "What cannot be seen with natural eyes, can be perceived with the eyes of prayer."

37. "Even when I feel like I am performing a self-talk, I am not; God is talking back with every pause in prayer."

38. "There is no time, no place and no posture with prayer."

39. "Not all prayer is equal; only praying to the God of our Lord Jesus Christ is not only symbolic gesture."

40. "What's spiritual success? It's being madly, madly, madly in love with Christ, His Words, and God's will."

41. "Once God saves you, He cannot take away your salvation. You can't lose your salvation, either, because you never gained it in the first place."

42. "There is no other way to say it, you can choose to believe in whatever you want or not to believe at all, but to believe that there is no God, is folly."

43. "Pray to God in faith whenever you can, however you can, with whomsoever you can,

for whoever you can, and by whatever means you can."

44. "If you realize that the church or pastor you follow is becoming a "lover of money", run, run very fast before you sell your soul to the devil. God is not glorified because of money, power or material "blessings," no. God is glorified because you love Him and obey Him. If you serve under a Ministry where each day the leader is getting richer and richer and everybody else is getting poorer and poorer, you're a fool to remain there or think that your efforts will help you and your family. Get out before it's too late and start your own Ministry where even if you struggle, you know you're doing your purpose on earth and serving God without hypocrisy."

45. "Life is like a ship on a wide sea, prayer is the campus, faith is the anchor, without either nothing but shipwreck is in sight."

46. "You have heard it said and written time and time again, that prayer ought to be a lifestyle. It is true. Pray for and about everything, without ceasing. Even let your last heart-beat or breath, if possible, be a prayer to God. God is unrevealed to people who do not pray. But

QUOT-EBOS

God shows Himself real, strong, faithful, closer and adequate to those who pray to Him."

47. "I know that every prayer I pray will be answered; only that it can be 'yes' or 'no.'"

48. "Sometimes prayer is the highest revelation of the selfishness in our hearts; that is why it purifies the soul."

49. "Every unanswered prayer is a demonstration of God's mercy; He knows and loves me that much to let me have the answer to some prayers."

50. "If it was not for prayer, I world have suffered heart attack, I would have been extremely distressed, and I would have died young."

51. "I influence important decisions and I rule my world through prayer; it is no wonder Paul said, 'Pray without ceasing.'"

52. "Prayer is the clearest way God invented to enable humans reshape events and matters on earth. I can pray that a situation works in a certain way, and it does; I can pray that things become a certain way, and they do."

53. "Faith is a tool. It connects the mortals to the immortals, temporal to divine and material to spiritual. Prayer is a gift. It translates faith into reality. With faith and prayer in combination, mortals become immortals, temporal touches the divine and material reaches spiritual invincibility."

54. "Prayer guarantees absolute peace and tranquility."

55. "Called by any other name, prayer is a wish, a desire, a want, a need, hope, an aspiration, a yearning, a longing, ambition, an objective, an aim, a dream, a determination, a craving, a hunger for, an intention, a goal, a purpose, a reason, or a motivation."

56. "The mystery of prayer is that it is an evidence of grace; we have all prayed to God or to something, and we have all received the gift of living."

23 | LOVE AND FAMILY

1. "Changing your spouse is simple if you first change *you*."

2. "The biggest challenge of any relationship, marriage or not, is selfishness: If the 'me' in the relationship is replaced by the 'us' or 'we', many relationships would be excellent."

3. "It's amazing that men think women are to blame for the break up in relationships, and women think that men are to blame. There is only one person to blame, you."

4. "It does not matter whether you planned the pregnancy or not, but when the child is conceived, it is your responsibility to take care of the child with purpose."

5. "Women usually respect a man who relentlessly demonstrate love for them."

6. "No matter how your man married or proposed you (if you're married to him), give him a benefit of doubt (and believe in him) when he fails or messes up or sins; You're the only one he calls, "My wife."

7. "Again, and again, God's love defeats me: How that His eyes which see me sin, look on me with mercy and watch me rise again."

8. "The danger about religion is that it can poison the mind so that you only see one way, my way. Love, however, is reasonable. Religion enslaves; love liberates."

9. "A man's greatest weakness is his wife; a woman's greatest strength is her husband."

10. "Love is painful. It entails sacrifice. It demands our undivided attention. It calls for bravery. It needs no negotiation. Love is hard work. And here is the test: Love is mostly true if you need no favor in turn, you're willing to choose the weak over the powerful, and you easily associate with the poor and don't despise them when the rich show up."

11. "There are certain things that cannot grow without love. Marriage is one of those things."

12. "You cannot erase the failure of failing to be there for your children when they are young. You can only wish you did it differently."

13. "The best blessing is from one's father, everything else is in between."

14. "Each day, work very hard to love those around you, to help them in ways that cause you discomfort. First love your spouse (you cannot claim to love your neighbor if you don't love your spouse); then love your neighbor (your neighbor is every other person you encounter other than you); and last, coming from these two, you will love the world. Every person is selfish (wanting very much to outsmart others, outdo others and be better than others) but love says, 'If you are better than me, I rejoice because it makes you happy!' That's why the greatest love on earth is when you are able to love your worst enemy."

15. "'He who is forgiven more loves more is a principle. Do you know that if you

forgive your partner in any relationship, they will love you much? Therefore, if you want that man/woman to love you unconditionally, have a habit of forgiving them of all faults unconditionally."

16. "RULE OF LOVE #1: A woman is like a jewelry of rare quality which when a man finds, he must treasure and end his search. Love keeps it durable; and romance polishes it brightly constantly."

17. "RULE OF LOVE #2: "Don't ask what your partner should do for you. Rather, think about, plan, and ask what you must do for them. In a relationship, if you make your partner happy, your happiness is guaranteed, if not now, then in the future in some way."

18. "RULE OF LOVE #3: "What you highlight is what you will see first. So, if you look for the best in your partner, you will find them."

19. "RULE OF LOVE #4: "If it ever passed your mind that, if necessary, you can die for your partner (take their bullet, as it were), then you can proudly

say, 'I love you.' Anything else is simply matters of flesh; anyone can easily say they love someone if its only beauty, money, sex or privilege they seek."

20. "RULE OF LOVE #5: "Always give into the relationship more than what you get out of it. If you give less and receive more, your relationship is in danger; if you give what you receive, your relationship will be average; if you give more than what you expect in return, you will find true satisfaction and lasting happiness."

21. "RULE OF LOVE #6: "If you can love what you can't see or touch, you have love that will last the test of time. If you love your partner heart, you have true and unshakable love; if you love their things and achievements, you have frail and fake love; if you love their body only, you have no love for them."

22. "RULE OF LOVE #7: "Love is like honey and a rose flower. Honey, the sweetest and healthiest natural product, is made by potentially deadly bees.

Roses, unarguably, the most beautiful natural auras, contain potentially painful thorns. You can't have honey without carefully negotiating the bees, and neither can you have roses without braving thorns. Our partners are both sweet and beautiful. To successfully enjoy them, we must handle the relationship with: (1) attention and care; (2) knowledge and understanding; (3) tenderness and toughness. A successful relationship (honey and roses) requires you to tender it with care and attention to your partner; understanding their weaknesses and strengths and knowing who they are to avoid offending; and being gentle with them as well as tough against forces that may interfere or destroy your relationship."

23. "RULE OF LOVE #8: "It is not your job to change your partner; it is, rather, if necessary, your duty to change. In the first place you loved them just for who they were, leave it that way. Everyone loves to be who they are; once your partner feels free to be who they are in your presence, they have found a true partner."

24. "RULE OF LOVE #9: "Money or sex or incompatibility does not destroy relationships. Personality differences do no, either. Children will not destroy relationships and neither are in-laws or former lovers. What does, more than all these, are words. Hurried, hasty, uncalculated, and unwise words or lack of communication can damage a relationship beyond repair. To sustain a good relationship, it is vital to listen to each other; use graceful language or talk less if possible; and never say something in anger which you will regret in happy times. Don't degrade, insult, belittle or humiliate your partner, in private or in public."

25. "RULE OF LOVE #10: "Your relationship will be most fulfilling when it is endeared and not endured. Play together, more often. Laugh together, always. Touch, hold hands, and be fun with each other, many times over. Meet each other's physical needs, if possible. And abuse each other, never."

26. "RULE OF LOVE #11: "There is something very endearing in forgiving the misdeeds of your partner. In a relationship, a grudge can be a small poison that can lead to a potentially good partnership eroding. To be able to forgive each other, partners should try hard to avoid situations in which offence is not an act of will. To offend one another deliberately and expect to be forgiven each time, is like drinking poison and calling it juice."

27. "RULE OF LOVE #12: "Love and marriage are like a marathon sprint on a hilly terrain. There is no relationship without ups and downs; there is nothing like a perfect relationship because we are all fallen beings. Therefore, it is not a matter of if there will be misunderstandings, quarrels, differences, upsets, disappointments, stress, anger, disagreements, failures, harsh words exchanged, and sometimes even fights. It is a matter of how you deal with those undesirables and use them as stepping stones to a desirable future that counts. The mantra is: Don't quit because the going gets tough; rather, endure,

QUOT-EBOS

negotiate and overcome all the huddles. And like purely refined gold, your relationship will come out sweet and rosy."

28. "RULE OF LOVE #13: "Finally, love her or him – the only obligation required to make any relationship work. It only matters that you love them, no excuses – don't worry about their weaknesses, issues or problems – love. Love them for his good things and for their bad things. Just love. Your relationship is guaranteed to survive, succeed, flourish, bear fruit, win, produce great results and endures to the end with happiness, joy and fulfilment where only love is. When you don't love in a love relationship, you only remain with pain, anger, disappointment and confusion. How much love should you give your partner – everything."

29. "RULE OF LOVE #14: "Make love happen."

30. "Your spouse earned your respect the day he/she married you; now ask him/her to keep the promise."

31. "Men and women, isn't it hypocrisy that you spend time 'liking' other people on FB, but you don't do the same for your spouse?"

32. "Never ever overlook your wife's looks, even when she's not as presentable, find something to praise."

33. "Never ever embarrass your husband because you are making more money; men don't like to look less."

34. "Don't think that another man or priest or pastor can fix your marriage; if you don't, you'll lose it."

35. "No matter how sophisticated women may be, they always long to know every day, that the husband still loves them."

36. "Any marriage can revive, all it takes is the husband saying those three words: 'I love you," consistently and meaningfully."

QUOT-EBOS

37. "Your parents can't know and don't need to know everything going on in your bedroom with your spouse."

38. "You, the wife, must sell your husband with pride, elegance and commitment; you're the number 1 promoter of your husband's image."

39. "As far as you're concerned, your wife can't do any wrong in public; but it's your job to correct her privately."

40. "No matter how tempted, don't tell your wife's problems to anyone, unless on mutual consent."

41. "No matter how tempted, don't tell your husband's problems to anyone, unless on mutual consent."

42. "There are blessings in love."

43. "Love makes waiting possible."

44. "Where love is, mercy shows up."

45. "A slave of love is richer than a master of hate."

46. "Love bears no grudge against its neighbor."

47. "Love deals well with a stranger near as with a friend afar."

48. "The beginning of love is to keep the commandments."

49. "Love is made of three parts: heart, soul and strength."

50. "Love is never measured in numbers."

51. "When love is pregnant; she gives birth to happiness."

52. "Love is the highest quality for any promotion."

53. "Love, is biased towards favor."

54. "As a campus is to a marine, so is love to a stranger."

55. "Love is constant."

56. "The love for the *Divine* brings rain."

57. "Love never let go."

58. "As gold in a furnace, so love is tested."

59. "Love never let go."

60. "As gold in a furnace, so love is tested."

61. "Love adds."

62. "Love is life."

63. "Love multiplies."

64. "Love lengthens your day."

65. "Love serves."

66. "Love is hard work."

67. "Those who love are like the sun in its strength."

68. "Where love is there the heart is."

69. "Love and delight are twins."

70. "Love is wonderful, pleasant altogether."

71. "If you receive hate for love, simply pray."

72. "Do not love because of; Rather love in spite of."

73. "What you meditate on most, perhaps you love it the most."

74. "Love is never double-minded."

75. "Let your life be a love-letter."

76. "Love and gold are both dear, the former is never rare."

77. "Make love one of your customs, and you be free of all charges."

78. "Lovely people are refreshing."

79. "When love shows up; lying escapes through the window."

80. "When you love what God loves, you prosper."

81. "To the extent to which love is abused, to that extend does it become hatred."

82. "Love is the wheel of the heart."

83. "Love is the cure for hatred."

84. "Love is a description and not a one-word answer."

85. "Love sees no flaws in others."

86. "In the eyes of love, everything is perfect."

87. "This is wherein love and death are similar: both are hard to defeat."

88. "The thirst of love cannot be quenched by many waters."

89. "Floods cannot drown love; it floats."

90. "Even over troubles, love floats."

91. "Love qualifies servants into sons."

92. "Love and justice are two sides of the same coin; in between lies the thin line of mercy."

93. "He that pursues love and pity shall see many days."

94. "The face of love is never distorted by pain or gain."

95. "Let your love be predictable."

96. "Love not that which you will live to regret."

97. "Love is the only thing that lasts longer than forever."

98. "Let the time to love be every time."

99. "You are commanded not to cheapen love."

100. "Let your mouth confess that which your heart loves."

101. "Love one woman; others like."

102. "Do not love dishonor."

103. "There is something gentle about love."

104. "Love with no strings attached."

105. "Love and be humble."

106. "Love sings and love is glad."

107. "In all your loving, love truth."

108. "Love knows no enemy and it is the most powerful force on earth."

109. "Rewards await those who love those who hate them."

110. "When you love your master, you destroy the boss in him."

111. "Love yourself first; then your neighbor as yourself."

112. "First, love God first. Or you can begin at first."

113. "All the hopelessness in the world can be cured, if only the antidote is love."

114. "Love is definitely better than law; when you love you are bound by no rules."

115. "Love gives hope, so much that you believe you can fly."

116. "When you are in love, all surroundings are roses, all stones are golden, and all things are possible."

117. "If you feel like life doesn't have your best interest any more, don't commit suicide, simply find someone who loves you, and you will live again."

118. "Slide delicately into the small spaces of life, and love, and in that moment, you are a winner, a champion, a master of your own destiny."

119. "If you love a woman, and she loves you back, mutually, enjoy every moment together - you will notice that you have the power to extend your life."

120. "Don't be in a hurry to nurture love, it invigorates life everywhere it passes."

121. "Investigators will find no fault in you, if you have love in you."

122. "Love awakens the flowers of youth, energizes the sleeping virtues, regenerates the thinning cells, and widens your shrinking faculties. Love is more powerful than death, because, unlike death, love leaves marks of delight

in its paths, so that even when you are not able to be saved from the jaws of death, your memories will grow wings and fly into an azure firmament, all too glorious to imagine and too transcendental to describe. Oh, love, you make everything, just things."

123. "Love is most remembered when the object of love was gentler, mellower, and softer. Love is least memorialized when a woman is grumpier, angrier, irritable and always demanding. A woman who only loves because of the things you do for her, is like a snake with two heads. It bites you with one and tenderizes you with the other. It kills you quickly with its poison and keeps you long enough to suffer from its venom. It kisses you with lips silhouettes of deadly acid and melts you down the journey you will never have a chance to return to life. You are a fool if you think that you will ever be yourself again. When you get your first opening, slide into it like a slimming snail; leave your pouch behind, even if you should melt into the landless terrains. You are better off without her. For sure, fools mistake beauty for grace,

and to its virulent mixture they will speedily succumb."

124. "It is the honor of a woman to love only one man at a time. It is the pleasure of men to entertain more than two women at the same time. It takes courage and self-control to remain with only one. Both sides must be willing to trade off and make sacrifices."

125. "Love is a mystery; marriage is an enigma. When you love a woman, you feel liberated. When you marry her, you feel imprisoned? If you should not marry her, love may die. If you marry her, love may turn into hate. Oh, wretched me, should I love her and not marry her so that love may survive, or should I marry her and risk love being turned into a weapon of hate?"

126. "A woman is best served with a dish of love mixed with patience. The best brew for a man is the one with the forms of reason. If the man is weak and allows the woman to dictate terms, he will soon realize that he has no honor among

peers. If the woman does not monitor her man's whereabouts, she would wake up single and alone. Love, therefore, can only blossom with restraints."

127. "It is easier to start a love affair than to end one. The beginning may be pleasurable, but the end always brings tears. Every love will end in nothing just like every life ends in death. The best time to love and nurture and care and thrill is now. The end shall surely come, and laughter shall be turned into mourning. But the memories of love shall live forever, like a dry rose when all the petals are blown away and the thorns get sharper, but its wonderful scents blend evenly and its aroma lends to the survivor a saintly pillow on which to lay her head in heavenly dreams."

128. "Love may be blind, but marriage is full sighted."

129. "It is not so easy to know whether a woman loves a man or she just needs him for another reason."

130. "There are many things that define beauty, facial appearance is the least among them."

131. "The greatest measure of a love affair is time – if the affair remains standing after many attacks, you know it was love."

132. "You can discern love if you first know the heart."

133. "If you haste into sex with a woman you think you love, the propensity to derailing the relationship only grows."

134. "Sex always happens; love may not."

135. "Patience is the shortest distance to true love."

136. "Love does not die; it may only be submerged by many forces."

137. "The love that is rushed may be compared to eating unripe pawpaw."

138. "When love is disappointed, the heart needs time to be ready for another."

139. "If the husband is a race-runner, the wife's job is keep cheering him and pointing him towards the finishing line."

140. "If the woman is a kite, the man's job is keep holding onto the rope so that the kite flies freely and does not fall."

141. "What keeps happiness in a marriage or relationship is constant tolerance and forgiveness."

142. "First give your greatest energy to God, then and equally to your spouse, and if there is anything left, give it for others."

143. "Don't love your sister-in-Christ or brother-in-Christ or your pastor or priest more than you love your spouse."

144. "It's the job of a church to wed people, not to divorce people or to tell them whom to marry."

145. "All men must strive to spend at least one minute more time with their spouse than they spend with their business, job or charity."

146. "If you are a married man, God doesn't want you to feed the whole world before you feed your wife, and children."

147. "If your confidence in marriage comes from your salary or the job title of your partner or your house or car - you're a prisoner."

148. "Discover and attempt many ways in which you can achieve perfect intimacy, with your spouse - if you don't, you'll soon be bored."

149. "If your choice for spouse is characterized more by 'good looks,' 'handsomeness,' 'beauty,' or 'perfection,' you're not ready for marriage yet."

150. "A Christian man's first spiritual responsibility is to lead his wife in Bible study – and to pray for her often."

151. "If marriage is sustained because of children or if it breaks because of lack of them, it was never a love relationship."

152. "Never treat your husband like your father or your wife like your mother - it's called incest."

153. "If you have a habit of dressing inappropriately so that men can clearly see your private assets, men will not respect your body in the end."

154. "If your glory is in your beauty, and your power is in your strength, your relationship is dead on arrival."

155. "No woman wants to linger with a man who doesn't complement her; no man wants to return to a home with a talkative wife."

156. "Divorce is preferable to murder."

157. "You shouldn't complain about or criticize your wife publicly, it reflects poorly on your overall sense of judgment."

158. "A husband is like a hired lawyer, if he stops to protect your interests, fire him."

159. "There is nothing like starving your man sexually, you may just give him more reasons to go out with other women."

160. "Even if your wife has a better job than you, the primary responsibility to fend for the family is the man's."

161. "Even if in your heart you know your husband is sexually worse than your previous men, don't vocalize it or you will kill the marriage."

162. "Love your wife for who she is - never, ever, or even imply, comparing her to another woman."

163. "The greatest weapon a woman has in order to guard her relationship is jealousy - do not discourage her from it."

164. "Men must pay attention to the tiny, small things about their wives - even if the woman does not respond favorably."

165. "When a woman is dressed up more to be praised by other men rather than by her own husband, she may be unfulfilled."

166. "The sign that your marriage may be dying is when your love-making becomes faster, shorter and quicker or doesn't exist at all."

167. "Your size, height or length doesn't matter, what satisfies in a relationship is that you are loved despite your limitations."

168. "Don't divorce the woman because of sexual techniques; when you learn sex together, its sweeter and lasts longer."

169. "When do you know that a marriage has survived? When a woman starts to

respect her husband, and the man starts to intentionally submit to his wife."

170. "A lazy husband and a man who uses money to control his wife is called a loser."

171. "If a woman begins to use sex as a weapon in marriage, run before your soul is sold to Satan."

172. "If you discern that the spirits of love and submission have died, work hard to restore, otherwise divorce."

173. "A relationship becomes strong when love becomes a choice, and not a feeling."

174. "If marriage was a rose flower, the woman is the petals; the man is the thorns."

175. "In a healthy relationship, a man makes more statements, a woman asks more questions, not the other way."

176. "Women must resist temptations to lead or dominate their husbands; men must be leaders in their marriages."

177. "A marriage where the husband loves the wife unconditionally, will survive."

178. "Any marriage where the wife allows the husband to lead or head will succeed."

179. "Sex in marriage is not barter system; it's a core term of the covenant."

180. "The easiest way to permanently stop something is to kill it - so, why don't you 'kill him with love' so he stops looking at other pretties."

181. "Sex in marriage is not secondary to your career or professional pursuits; it is the first priority."

182. "If a woman says more often that, 'I am tired,' to engage in marital sex, she devalues marriage."

183. "The secret to a long, fulfilling and treasured sexual enjoyment in marriage, is not to use it or do it as a pass-time."

184. "I am now in my mid-ages, and I have never seen a woman who respected herself not respected by wise men."

185. "The more tenderly and softly you treat your women, the stronger she becomes – the only place where weakness is a strength."

186. "It's the glory of women to hesitate to say, 'Yes' to a marriage proposal; it is the pleasure of men to chase after love for as long."

187. "No-one needs experience with sex, it rolls out naturally like breastfeeding."

188. "The sign that we have lost our values, is when you see sex portrayed as cheap and easily accessible in every scene of cinematic pictures."

189. "You gain nothing but pain thinking that you can enjoy sex before marriage."

190. "God, gods, even idols know the value of sexual purity before marriage, who are you not to."

191. "If people tell you to be promiscuous to get sexual experience, it's like chewing gum, soon it will lose its taste."

192. "No man who married a virgin never thought he gained gold; there is no better wedding gift."

193. "The more sex you have with people the less experienced sexually you become; the less the better, none before marriage the best."

194. "Unforgiveness connects you to the source of your pain and poison; forgiveness keeps you away from their hold on you."

195. "Lead your wife, for God's sake, or God will judge you if she leads you astray - remember Adam."

196. "There is more hope for a fool than for a man who thinks that his wife will always be in a mood for sex."

197. "If you have a husband, don't deny him sex arbitrarily - you may drive a foolish one into pornography and immorality."

198. "Most pastor's wives shouldn't work in church, just like you don't marry a doctor and think that you'll work in the hospital."

199. "To think that you will be happy if you marry a pastor, is like hiding gold in sand and thinking that it will be safe."

200. "Please don't be a bad wife because you're married to a pastor, and don't be a bad pastor because you're married to a bad wife."

201. "Why do those who went through divorce later have stronger marriages?

Partly because they learned how it does not work."

202. "It takes courage to divorce, if you see a divorced woman or man, you have seen how courage looks like in person."

203. "If you want your marriage to last longer or forever, decide to take the word 'divorce' out of your marriage vocabulary."

204. "Women, don't despise a man who tells you he loves you, to many men, that takes courage to utter."

205. "Women, you're commanded to submit to only one man called a 'husband,' to all men, you are an equal."

206. "It is a foolish woman who rebukes her man in public, in secret a rebuke from your woman is golden flakes."

207. "In every culture, desired men are those who are soft to their woman and hard on everyone else, and not the other way around."

QUOT-EBOS

208. "Don't define a real man by physical features, you will soon regret, rather, define one by character, integrity and industry."

209. "Don't marry a man who has not invested in a trade called 'wisdom.'"

210. "If you find a wise and diligent woman married to a stupid, unwise man, she has more regrets than a tiger than misses its prey."

211. "I find it troubling why beautiful, wise and respectable women fall for foolish, irresponsible men."

212. "If the only reason you want to marry a woman is because you want sex with her, you're a total fool."

213. "Always listen to your woman, but only act on wise things she says."

214. "If women cause you to stumble often, you are a boy in your mind."

215. "Real men take control; foolish men lose control."

216. "How does Christ love the church - He purifies it with the Word, a husband, too, must love his wife, saying good things about her, often."

217. "How does Christ love the church - He forgives it all day long - that's how a husband ought to be and do to his wife."

218. "When it comes to sex, all women are the same in the end; don't despise your wife thinking another woman will be better."

219. "If your wife makes all important decisions in your marriage, there are two women living in that home."

220. "Only fools think that you cannot reprimand that which you love; actually, the more you are loved, the more you'll be corrected."

221. "Even when you tell your wife that she is dead wrong, you are very much alive in love with her."

222. "The balance between love and leadership is the material real men are made of in regards to marriage."

223. "Women are like little puppies, love and play with them so long as they behave but correct them when you see unreasonable behavior."

224. "If you can't lead, care and correct a woman, you may not be fit to get married yet."

225. "Graveyards grow with more dead people added; be certain that your church is not expanding due to more spiritually dead souls."

226. "If you don't believe in God, I can't trust you - you can't claim to love a creature more than its Creator."

227. "Women's breasts and men's *peni* have the same function - they both release life-giving fluids."

228. "The weakest link in a human anatomy is the genitalia, do not expose it cheaply or you will fall easily."

229. "The only position higher than the president's is your family."

230. "You should not put your trust in anything that dies, even if it's called a 'bishop.'"

231. "The weaker with women your husband is, the more you must love him."

232. "If you spend all your life in one place, you will limit what God can do through you."

233. "To women, sex is like groundnuts, they discard the skin and keep the seeds."

234. "To men, sex may be like football, they kick it and wait for another pass."

235. "You're either stupid or a fool if you think that a married man with children will make you first; you're third in line."

236. "If you think that you will stop to lust after women when you get married, there is more hope for Satan to enter Heaven than for you."

237. "If you think that your husband must make you happy, you have wasted half of your life."

238. "Even a fool is king if he or she pays herself."

239. "If your goal is to gain a higher salary, you are a servant or at least a slave; if you think of paying yourself, you're a boss."

240. "If you don't think of rising higher than your boss, you're doing other people's purpose."

241. "Men think in terms of sex; women in terms of babies – both are right."

242. "If you haven't smiled, laughed or danced in a long time, death may be better to you than life."

243. "If you think about life in terms of money, you will always be behind, think of it in terms of love, you will be far ahead."

244. "If you look at yourself and love what you see, people will also love how you look."

245. "When I cared what people would think, I accomplished nothing; when I cared what God would think, I made progress."

246. "The biggest enemy in the world is not Satan, it's ignorance."

247. "Women are nature's natural jewels; wise men tender all their curves heartly and gently, and adore all their graces meticulously."

248. "It is not wrong to promote yourself, if you do it in good faith."

249. "Girl children are like scented perfume; worn in moderation, they effuse the most elevated fragrance."

250. "Love speaks graciously of others, smooths the rough edges of comrades, gently caresses painful abscesses of life, sacrificially gives itself for other's comfort, and boldly kisses the impertinences of those who least receive care."

251. "The greatest gift a man can receive is that which combines both beauty and grace in the same person."

252. " Train up a child in the way he should go, and when he is old he will not depart from it" (Proverbs 22:6, Bible).

253. "Foolishness is bound up in the heart of a child, but the rod of discipline drives it far from him," (Proverbs 22:15, Bible).

254. "Both fand love have a place in the community called family; love takes a whip and love measures the degree of implementation."

255. "Love is the most powerful force on earth."

24 | HOPE

1. "Hope is the only weapon that defeats death."

2. "If hope comes between you and death, death will flee."

3. "Hope is always available in the world; your job is to find it."

4. "Hope never loses you, you are the one who loses hope, instead."

5. "Where there is hope, there is life."

6. "Hope makes abstract concepts become things."

7. "There is nothing that hope has failed to create."

8. "The voice of hope searches the past, saves the present, and sustains the future."

9. "First hope, then faith."

10. "Never leave hope, even if you are drowning."

11. "You can always find hope if you take time to look."

12. "Hope never disappoints once you make an appointment with it."

13. "Hope will search heaven and hell to bring you what you agreed with it to."

14. "Even the strongest medicine will fail without hope."

15. "With hope, the future is as clear and certain as the past."

16. "Circumstances will make your life harder; hope will make it easier."

17. "Hope will extend your years and postpone death."

18. "Hope is neutral – it makes both bad and good come true."

19. "Where there is hope, strategies and tactics become alive."

20. "With hope, you may lose a battle but win the war."

21. "Kingdoms are held together by hope, and destroyed by doubt."

22. "Don't give someone money before you give them hope, it'll be squandered."

23. "The easiest way to kill anything, is to first separate it from hope."

24. "Even the mighty fall, when they lose hope."

25. "With hope, death is not the end, it is the beginning."

26. "Faith is great, hope is greater, and love is the greatest."

27. "The best plans are those which give rise to hope."

28. "Hope is synonymous with a future."

29. "Hope is blind to directions; it is your duty to set it on the right trajectory."

30. "Work must be produced by faith, labor prompted by love, and endurance inspired by hope."

31. "Hope takes the shape of its master."

32. "If your hope is in God, you will reap eternal life."

33. "You can hope in anything; hope doesn't choose whom to obey."

34. "Hope loves those who love it; and is far away from those who doubt."

35. "Hope all the way."

36. "If you lose hope, you can find it again, if you don't quit."

37. "The difference between hope and faith; hope doesn't need faith, but faith does need hope."

38. "Hope is neither a believer nor a non-believer; it's a-believer."

39. "Christ is the hope of glory."

40. "Education, knowledge and enlightenment bring hope."

41. "Like money, hope is valuable, if you don't keep it with care, it vanishes."

42. "Hope is delicate and slippery, hold on to it unswervingly."

43. "Hope renews one's strength in the Lord."

44. "The hope of the ungodly has a future, but a bad future."

45. "The hope of the godly is unfailing love."

46. "Those who have hope, praise God more and more."

47. "Hope in God's word, makes waiting possible."

48. "One thing hope never does for its client; it never puts them to shame."

49. "If you already have it, don't hope for it; rather, hope for what is not."

50. "Hope is currency, the more you have, the richer you are."

51. "If your God never gives you hope, it is a dead god."

52. "Integrity effuses hope."

53. "Hope saves."

54. "A good night sleep is only possible because of hope for tomorrow."

55. "Hope ignores the past, and believes in the future."

56. "With hope, rivers won't sweep you away, fires won't burn you up, and flames won't set you ablaze."

57. "To set your mind on things above, is to have hope."

58. "Hope is like a mustard seed; it grows into a big plant."

59. "Hope makes work pleasant."

60. "It is the glory of men to hope; it is the delight of God to bring the victory."

61. "Courage and heroism dance to the tune of hope."

62. "Hope for big things, bigger than your strength, and hope will work double."

63. "Hope does not come from the mountains; it comes from within and above you."

64. "If you don't say yes to hope, hope will say no to you."

65. "There is a dead hope and a living hope; the later leads to true riches."

66. "Hope gives birth post-menopause."

67. "Shadows will always hope, so long as the sun remains."

68. "The hope of smoke is fire, that of shadow is the light, and of man, is the unseen reality."

69. "The poor have hope."

70. "If you can pray, God can grant you what you hope for."

71. "Hope for something before you pray."

72. "Where there is hope, there is security and safety."

73. "If you put your hope in God's never-ending love, He will delight in you."

74. "If you postpone hope, your heart will get sick."

75. "Ultimately, all mankind hope for the glory of God."

QUOT-EBOS

76. "Hope engineers things only envisioned by wishes."

77. "Hope is like a campus; lose it and you lose direction."

78. "Hope makes gods and immortals equal; with it they conquer the future."

79. "Anything that you allow to kill your hope, loads over you."

80. "Never go to war or be involved in a war without hope alongside you."

81. "Give hope the first place in your future schedule."

82. "Look for hope, everywhere."

83. "Those who have hope may go down, but they always end up above."

84. "Hope and endurance are related; they both reach the finishing line."

85. "Hope shines brightest when it is darkest."

86. "No matter how tough the task is, where there is hope and perseverance, there is a solution."

87. "Don't write anyone off who has hope."

88. "Hope and positive expectation are two sides of the same coin; you can't have one without the other."

89. "'For I know the plans I have for you,' declares the LORD, 'plans to prosper you and not to harm you, plans to give you hope and a future.'"

90. "Hope breeds confidence."

91. "There may be many enemies in the journey of progress, but with hope, they can all be defeated."

92. "The first last weapon a soldier must secure and the last he must lose is called hope."

93. "If you can't hope for anything, you won't have faith to endure and love to wait."

94. "Determination produces hope which is essential in the fulfilment of the vision. Because life is full of ups and downs, living without hope is dangerous."

95. "The law of importunity simply states: 'Quitters are not winners.'"

25 | ACTIONS

1. "There are seeds in anyone's actions."

2. "What is slavery? It's doing something for somebody without earning anything."

3. "There is little love in what you say; much love is in what you do."

4. "You can say all you want, but it's what you do that justifies or denigrates you. It is what you do, not what you say, that will meet people's needs."

5. "If you find that you are working hard, doing more and laboring long hours, but you're getting little or nothing, quit."

6. "You can change anything if you do something."

7. "Satan likes two kinds of people: Those who do nothing, and those who do something that's not God's will."

8. "Anything or anyone who says you can't, is not your friend."

9. "Anywhere there is more land than people, there is more to do."

10. "Don't make begging a habit, unless it is begging from God."

11. "How do you run away from laziness? By doing the things laziness hates."

12. "How do you run away from poverty? By doing the things poverty hates."

13. "If you only did one percent of what you read about money,

you would have more money in your account."

14. "Spend less time commenting on good ideas, take more time experimenting on what they suggest."

15. "A person who spends more time doing than listening, is also richer, unless listening is his career."

16. "Even disappointment and failure are successes if you did something you failed in."

17. "If you don't know what to do, help someone else win."

18. "Rewarding actions have three goals: Making money; serving humanity; or glorying God. Anything else is a waste."

19. "A bush is only a garden that has not been tended."

20. "Beauty becomes ugly if nothing is done to improve it."

21. "If you don't cultivate your ground, nothing but weeds will grow on it."

22. "Money follows those who do something with it."

23. "Anyone who is better than you, is only so because she did something extra."

24. "Nothing happens when you do nothing; it is known as a 'no.'"

25. "Something happens when you do something; it is known as a 'some.'"

26. "After King David had done God's will, he died."

QUOT-EBOS

27. "Take actions, even if they are baby steps."

28. "God will take away from you if you do nothing with what he Has given you."

29. "Rejected once, try twice; rejected twice, try four times."

30. "The heart is always beating, so that your hands can keep doing."

31. "If you could do as much as you talk, you would be more prosperous."

32. "If your heart stops, we call it death; if your brain stops, we call it legally dead; when you do nothing, who are you?"

33. "We know something has life only when it does something with a part of its body."

34. "Do something with everything God gave you, with everything."

35. "Tell me, what are you doing now?"

36. "If you can put into action 99 percent of ideas and thoughts that come to your mind, you would have achieved at least 50 percent."

37. "Procrastination is anti-prognostication."

38. "Even if you fail, actions are still worth it."

39. "Laziness is the inability to do anything with one's available time and resources."

40. "Champions, winners, victors and overcomers have one thing in common, they did it."

41. "Time is meaningless if nothing is being done."

42. "Resting is the reward of actions actually done."

43. "I have failed in 100 percent of the chances I never took."

44. "I have succeeded in zero percent of the targets I never took."

45. "Even a well-prepared meal will be tasteless, unless it is eaten."

46. "In the beginning, God did something."

47. "The only time doing nothing has value, is before you are born."

48. "All who succeed have one thing in common; they do."

49. "Sometimes an idea dies because of lack of action."

50. "The fear of doing has hindered success more than the bravery of hope."

51. "A man has both a brain and limbs, so that he must both think and do."

52. "Death is also defined as 'doing nothing.'"

53. "Think, plan, and do."

54. "A deed done, is more profitable than words said."

55. "Time is only managed by those who do."

56. "Jesus always said, 'come', 'go' and 'do.'"

57. "Take actions when you can, where you can, and if you can."

58. "Postponed actions lead to poverty."

59. "A wrong action taken is better than a good plan which was not implemented."

60. "If half of the world acted, half of the world's problems would have been solved."

61. "Don't do today's actions tomorrow."

62. "Vision and thinking are just the beginning; action makes it all happen."

63. "You cannot be convicted for a crime if action is absent."

64. "Even faith only works with action."

65. "Action is everything; even the best plans are nothing without action."

66. "It is not what happens to you: Bad, ugly, awful, nauseating, repugnant, disappointing, embarrassing, frustrating, failing, losing, shaming, excoriating, humbling, abusive, stone-walling, belittling, demeaning, heartbreaking, defeating, and etc. It is not where you live: Poor, undeveloped, unhygienic, dirty, neglected, and etc. It is not who

QUOT-EBOS

you are: Tall, short, fat, slim, African, European, American, Asian, Islander, educated, uneducated, learned or ignorant, young or old, male or female, exposed or local, married or divorced or single, and etc. It is not your tribe, your class, your culture, your language, your race, your caste, your position or lack thereof, your bank account or lack thereof, your status in the country, or etc. Not any one of these can bring you down and limit what you can do and be; If and when you decide to look above all your negatives, they become wings to help you fly higher to your desired destiny."

67. "Love is truly love when actions precede words."

68. "More deception is done by words, less by actions."

69. "Both wisdom and understanding live at the intersection of good conduct and meekness."

70. "Your light shines the brightest when you show good works more than when you say good words."

71. "The one who says, 'I will' and later changes her mind and says, 'I will not,'; and the one who says, 'I will not,' and later changes her mind and says, 'I will,' the later did the deed required to be approved."

72. "The definition of hypocrisy is professing to know either God or something, but the actions state otherwise."

73. "More than the many words Jesus said, it was that one act of dying on the Cross for people that brought salvation to all mankind; one action spoke louder than many words, so should we."

74. "You can quote many Scriptures *en* marathon, but unless you do deeds, your faith is questionable."

75. "For God so loved the world, that he gave."

76. "You can't rise up without doing, though you can fall without doing."

77. "Works are the spirits that give faith its power."

78. "Not everyone who says to me, 'Lord, Lord,' will enter the kingdom of heaven, but the one who does the will of my Father who is in heaven."[42]

79. "Why do you call me 'Lord, Lord,' and not do what I tell you?"[43]

80. "And whatever you do, in word or deed, do everything in the name of the Lord Jesus, giving thanks to God the Father through him."[44]

81. "Happy are those who do, and not just hear."

---

[42] Matthew 7:21
[43] Luke 6:45–46
[44] Colossians 3:17

82. "If you do more deeds, you will have less difficulties accounting for the many words you've spoken in the Day of Judgment."

83. "What is nobility? It is researching and finding out if what you have heard is, in fact, true."

84. "A true follower does the deeds of his master, and becomes like his master."

85. "Every good deed is lawful, anywhere on the globe."

86. "If you do the deeds of the kingdom first, everything else in the kingdom will be yours."

87. "When you are seen as you are, you become perfect."

88. "When you are loving and obedient, you are fit for any good work."

89. "Don't just do something, but also desire to do it."

90. "Believing in God is action, and, therefore, it is counted as righteousness."

91. "The ultimate goal of a follower is to become a leader."

92. "If someone is hungry, giving him a prayer is mockery."

93. "You cleanse your body by washing it with water; you cleanse your soul by confessing your sins."

94. "The only thing loftier than wisdom is the power of God."

95. "Tell me you know by doing."

96. "Any activity that requires the use of a tongue is very risky."

97. "Speech and anger are similar; they both require critical management."

98. "Whatever good reaches you, is from God, but whatever evil befalls you is from yourself."[45]

99. "Eat good things and do good deeds."[46]

---

[45] The Quran
[46] *Ibid.*

100. "Let none find fault with others; let none see the omissions and commissions of others. But let one see one's own acts, done and undone."[47]

101. "Vision without action is just a dream, action without vision just passes the time, and vision with action can change the world."[48]

102. "If you can't fly then run, if you can't run then walk, if you can't walk then crawl, but whatever you do you have to keep moving forward."[49]

---

[47] Buddha
[48] Nelson Mandela
[49] Martin Luther King Jr.

103. "Wherever you go, go with all your heart. The superior man acts before he speaks, and afterwards speaks according to his action. Wisdom, compassion, and courage are the three universally recognized moral qualities of men. What you do not want done to yourself, do not do to others."[50]

104. "The goal is not to be better than the other man, but your previous self. Happiness is not something ready-made. It comes from your own actions."[51]

---

[50] Confucius
[51] Dalai Lama

105. "Therefore, all things whatsoever ye that men would do to you: do ye even so to them."[52]

106. "On earth, nothing is superior to actions; miracles are subservient."

107. "Every time you do something, you produce something."

108. "Action has wheels; nouns have buttocks."

109. "Ask and it will be given to you; seek and you will find; knock and the door will be opened to you."[53]

---

[52] The Golden Rule
[53] Matthew 7:7

110. "A fool who does something profitable is smarter than a wise person who does nothing and loses."

111. "Take actions often, but always take well-thought-through actions."

112. "Actions are like swords. Well-chosen, gracious actions heal and bring joy. Actions which are meant to demean and offend others are like poisonous ingredients in a good-looking meal; they kill."

113. "Just like a sheathed sword does no harm, so are cleverly chosen actions."

114. "Good actions not done are like bad actions well done."

115. "A wise sage once posed this enigma: 'But what do you think? A man had two sons, and he came to the first and said, Son, go work today in the vineyard. And he answered, I will not; but afterward he regretted it and went. The man came to the second and said the same thing; and he answered, I will, sir; but he did not go. Which of the two did the will of his father? They said, 'The first.'"

26 | ANIMAL WISDOM

1. "Be like an African buffalo; avoid wounding other people emotionally lest you are attacked aggressively; but attack aggressively so you may protect your young."

2. "Be like a buffalo; though you may be short on eyesight and hearing, but you may use your strong sense of smell to compensate."

3. "So much as elephants choose maturity over vanity for leadership, so their memories are sharp as razor."

4. "Be like a polar bear; humble in looks, determined in attitude; and unafraid of anything."

5. "See far, be bored and strong, soar towards danger, fly high, re-energize and metamorphosize, but be gentle and attentive to your loved and young ones, like an eagle."

6. "Read people's emotions, be interested in new things and ideas, bond with loved ones, despise untrustworthy friendships, discern danger, discriminate in favor of family, earn your food, and take time to pet your loved ones, just like dogs do."

7. "Treasure your personal space, let your friendly presence be felt rather than only touched, esteem cleanliness, and be inquisitive to search and learn, just like cats do."

8. "Be sneaky, sly, cunning, and able to penetrate any system, like a fox."

9. "Be swift and also gracious, just like a gazelle."

10. "In your organization, perform like geese: Share a common goal; make your product or service visible; ask for help when needed; groom others for leadership; recognize the contributions of others

regularly; tend to the weak and vulnerable; and stick with the process until you reach your dream; just like geese do."

11. "The chimpanzee uses 66 distinct gestures to accomplish what human vocals do. If you can speak with gestures, you will make mistakes less, be sensitive twice, and establish lasting relationships thrice."

12. "Crows may not have strong enough teeth to crack nuts. So, they drop the seed along the road so that motor vehicles can crack the seeds for them. The best skill is the skill that uses the skills of other people to accomplish a task."

QUOT-EBOS

13. "Ants—they aren't strong, but they store up food all summer."[54]

14. "Hyraxes [rock badgers]—they aren't powerful, but they make their homes among the rocks."[55]

15. "Locusts—they have no king, but they march in formation."[56]

16. "Lizards—they are easy to catch, but they are found even in kings' palaces."[57]

17. "There are three things that are stately in their stride, and four that are impressive in their walk: A lion, mighty among

---

[54] Proverbs 30:25
[55] Proverbs 30:26
[56] Proverbs 30:27
[57] Proverbs 30:28

beasts, refusing to retreat before anything; a strutting rooster; a he-goat; and a king with his army around him."[58]

18. "There is not an animal that lives on the earth, nor a being that flies on its wings, but they form communities like you."[59]

19. "He, who injures living beings, is not noble. He is called noble because he is gentle and kind towards all living beings."[60]

20. "Humankind differs from the animals only by a little and most people throw that away."[61]

---

[58] Proverbs 30:29-31
[59] Quran 6:38
[60] Buddha
[61] Confucius

27 | MISCELLANOUS

1. "If you have an enemy, you have only three options: Run away, or make them your friend or eliminate them."

2. "All pain is temporary; joy lasts forever."

3. "As fire is hottest at the beginning and fades with time, so the drops of water weaken at the beginning and grow stronger with time."

4. "Patience is the first fruit of love and the last wall of defence in leadership."

5. "I have come to believe that small defeats are essential to a big victory."

6. "I know that happy news is not always good news; Jesus preferred the latter."

7. "What does it mean to be brave? It simply means that you have the courage to face up to negative circumstances that come your way."

8. "Surely character is forged in adversities, and the sweetest taste of victory comes to those who have experienced the worst bite of negative circumstances."

9. "Fear is the first enemy a general must defeat before they head out to battle."

10. "A little bit of stress is necessary; a lot of distress usurps morale."

QUOT-EBOS

11. "The greatest enemy of progress is doubt that we can't be. Defeat doubt, win destiny."

12. "Tough times make us; they shouldn't break us."

13. "A heart fares, cares and lives better and stronger when it is pure; a mind thinks progressively and inventively when it is at peace; our faculties exhibit order, creativity and accomplishment when they are clear; and a city or country is rich and has a strong economy when its environs and surroundings are sanitary and clean. Rich cities and nations are also clean. Poor cities and nations are usually dirty. Dirty cities and nations are likely to be corrupt places. Clean cities and nations are relatively less corrupt. A people with a dirty

culture (who don't care about their surroundings) also tolerate laziness, corruption and are normally lacking in productivity. To be whole or rich or have a strong economy, people and nations must first embrace a culture of cleanliness - pure hearts, peaceful minds, clear faculties, clean and sanitary homes and streets and cities. We can't do one while ignoring the other."

14. "Without a problem, there can never be a solution. And a solution, of course, is the end of the problem. So, the issue is not that there are problems, the issue is how do we turn the problem into a profit."

15. "If you can't quickly bury the disappointments, failures, mistakes, pains and embarrassments of yesterday,

you're not ready to conquer the future."

16. "Pain and poverty are only tolerable if they are means to a good end; for any other purpose, one has to do everything to escape both."

17. "Liberty and freedom are related terms which only become useful if the enslaver is threatened."

18. "Racism and racialization may not be differentiated, because where one is, the other lurks."

19. "Men don't struggle to love a submissive woman."

20. "A good exercise for the heart is to bend down and help another."

21. "When an average person puts in above average effort, he wins."

22. "Fools enjoy to be perceived as silent, but the wealth of the wise is in their words."

23. "You will eventually be promoted if you make others laugh and feel better about themselves."

24. "Achievement is not an event; it is a state of mind."

25. "At the end of your life, your success will be measured not by how much you made but by how you used what you made in the treatment of others."

26. "What is better than best? It is doing what is required, and to exceed it."

27. "Yes, there is a formula for success and promotion. Chance has very little to do with it. There could be other factors that may hinder our progress, but with this attitude we could eliminate those factors substantially. When you understand and define your assignment, you are performing at 100 percent. But in order to win the hearts of your seniors (bosses, clients, customers, or people) you need to do more. You need to excel. So, whatever you are doing, lead. Yes, leadership means being first, going ahead of the rest."

28. "Accept failure only if your next step is trying again."

29. "Saying 'Thank you' is the most unselfish human response –

every time you thank people you demonstrate that you're living for a larger cause, above self."

30. "All humans are born equal – and each individual is given a blank cheque at birth. It is what you think and say that either limits or pushes you forward."

31. "Life is like a game. In any game there are rules and guidelines. Winning means you play according to those rules. To win in any game that involve rules you need both the tangible and the intangible. Your intangible is your motivation. Your primary tangible includes your strategy and tactics. Play to win, no matter which opposition. Plan for your victories, then device a method of achieving them. When you begin the process to your

victory, do not throw away your confidence, your motivation – it will take you there. Even when you encounter impediments, keep your confidence, because once the storm has passed, you will reap the gold. That is how great leaders manage life."

32. "Five things you must protect and even fight for: (1) Your health - unless you are passed 70/80 years; (2) Your family - never allow anyone take advantage of your family; (3) Your relationship - don`t give up on your fight to protect your relationship; (4) Your job or business - no-one should destroy your job or business; (5) Your faith - let not the devil destroy what God has begun in your life."

33. "No matter how many times you get knocked down, keep getting up as long as there is strength in you."

34. "Go, do, act, make and create are action words. Gone, done, made and created are completed action words. A deed, a creation and an action are nouns of something completed. Make your action word a noun at the end of the day."

35. "'If I fail' are the three most dangerous words. They naturally lead to lethargy and laziness in that combination. 'I can succeed' are three most attractive words, because they attract whatever is desired. Instead of saying, 'If I fail,' try saying, 'I can succeed,' and you will."

36. "If we can say that we're alright with what we have and who we are, we can be free and happy. A lot of our anxieties, restlessness, and lack of fulfilment is because we are either not satisfied with what we have or not happy with who we are, or both. If we can take what we have, love it, polish it and use it; and then accept who we are, love ourselves just the way we are and stop being discontented and comparing to others, we can live happy and never regret we were born the way we were."

37. "If I am happy when another person succeeds, especially if that person is someone I least expect to succeed, I have learned the deepest art of loving my neighbor as I love myself. If I am happy when my worst

enemy fails or falls, I am not better than the devil himself."

38. "If the word 'Impossible' exists in 10 percent of one's thinking and conversations, that person is without doubt, lazy."

39. "One or three people won US$1.5 billion jackpot in January 2016. They instantly turned into millionaires. Never use the word 'impossible' in your vocabulary unless you want to say that, 'It is impossible not to be rich.'"

40. "In the beginning God worked, so that no human being should claim rights to laziness."

41. "When Adam and Eve sinned, they were perfect and lived in a perfect world. We are, however, born in an imperfect world and we sin. David was called 'A

man after God's heart after he had made serious mistakes and did terrible sins, not before that.'"

42. "The world is so constructed that if you wish to enjoy its pleasures, you must also endure its pains. Like it or not, you cannot have one without the other."

43. "Success is not measured by what you accomplish. It's measured by the opposition you encounter, and the courage with which you maintain your struggle against the odds."

44. "You'll find all things are difficult before they are easy."

45. "The greater your obstacles, the more glory in overcoming them."

46. "So, make up your mind before you start that sacrifice is part of the package."

47. "No pain, no gain; No thorns, no throne; No cross, no crown."

48. "We don't learn because we know but because we don't know. Our toughest critics are our greatest clue to our success."

49. "You will never know what you are capable of until you try. Don't let others define you, not even your wife or husband, your mother or father. You are like a rocket; you are unstoppable, and with God's

help, you will make it to the top."

50. "Even before modern industries learned about the concepts of re-use and re-cycle, God had that already figured out – forgiveness."

51. "People should not write your final script; you can write that for yourself. So, whether you failed, sinned, was disappointed, divorced, lost a job, became bankrupt, embarrassed, ashamed or rejected, the end is not yet. You can rise and become better than before those circumstances. Today, believe again, and begin, again on your way to better things."

52. "You are right, always, if you protect another's rights."

53. "Children are innocent. Whatever you see in them, good or bad, is you when you're not pretending."

54. "Anger is like a flickering flame; blow it up and it becomes a fire."

55. "There are only two genders – male and female – and you know you are not the other if you honor and treat the other as yourself."

56. "You know you are a useless man if you ignore and mistreat your woman."

57. "How do you know you're already dead, if you don't feel guilty when you abuse another person."

58. "Help the people you need to help *today*; give to the people

and causes you need to give to *today*; love the people around you *today*; care for things that matter more than today, *today*; and do, say and make the best things *today*. When it comes to life, nobody knows whether tomorrow will be yours, but you're sure of *today* – so become what you've intended to become *today*."

59. "When a person finds themselves doing what they should have done last year, (they are lucky to be alive this year) that's when it becomes failure."

60. "Itch not to hear a fellow human being has failed, but desire to help those who can't help themselves."

61. "The strong among us are only so because of the strength of us all, and the weakest among us is to receive more love and care."

62. "Failure is success when you did your best and your best was judged as not measuring up."

63. "What is humility? Humility is being broke and not be ashamed; being low and not feeling burdened; and being yourself and loving it."

64. "You're also a professor if everything you say and do help people in their professions."

65. "What do groups like Boko Haram, al-Qaeda, al-Shabaab, ISIS-K and ISIS have in common – it is not terror, it is not religion, and it is not geography, either. It is an idea. The only way to destroy a

people speaking the same language is to confuse their language and thwart their idea."

66. "Any Nigerian president, who fails to account for the girls captured by Boko Haram and bring the insurgent group to justice or punishment, has failed under Heaven."

67. "Don't join any group whose mission is the killing or torturing of innocent people; no matter the motivation, such groups are agents of evil."

68. "Anyone who preaches hate loves death."

69. "Always know what your enemy is doing."

70. "If you rise to the top by manipulation, you will fall quick and fast sooner rather than later; and if you hang in there long, you will live as though you have failed."

71. "The only thing you should not be tired of telling, is the truth."

72. "Seasons are a reminder that not all days are equal; on some days it rains, on others it shines, on another it is windy, and yet on another it may snow, yet it all answers to man's respite, to his pleasure or pain."

73. "The most important thing in life is not a thing; it's called people."

74. "Pleasure is good, only if it is pleasurable all the way."

75. "Whatever is lovely, pleasurable, happily, exciting, vibrant, cute, beautiful, good looking, excellent, admirable, pleasant, perfect, sweet, wealthy, healthy, magnificent, fabulous, glorious, gorgeous, tasty, fruitful, rich, attractive, enjoyable, delightful, gratifying, satisfying, honorable, impeccable, splendid, delicious, juicy, fair and sexy, and such others like these: Think, have, do and chase after such. But know that it is only relative to your taste."

76. "It is a lack of appreciation of God's generosity to deny yourself of the good things of life."

77. "You can't love God if you fail to love the good things of life,

because God made them and God is good."

78. "He is a wise person who recognizes that it is not bad to enjoy life."

79. "She who loves the Creator must also love His creation."

80. "Pleasure is always good if you are its master and not its slave."

81. "The best way to be encouraged is to encourage another."

82. "Men, even at their highest and best, are just as low and as least as the dust."

83. "Is it religion when color dictates the gala, tribe or race informs the grace, and injustice gives notice: If it is not love, nothing will stay above it."

84. "It is so refreshing that people know they are poor, even when they have never been rich; and the heart knows, and rejoices, when it has done something good."

85. "It is a sad shock to learn that just a few seconds before you pass away that all along there was never a *tomorrow*, only a *today*."

86. "Do the good you have always wanted to do *today*, *tomorrow* will never be."

87. "What you call *today* in North America, is called *yesterday* in Africa and *tomorrow* in the far Pacific Ocean."

88. "It is not complicated to practice medicine or law or accountancy, or any other popular professions, trades or careers: The only profession or trade or career that is complicated is the one which requires you to be all things to all people."

89. "There is nothing like a profession that is useless or unimportant; everything a person does if it earns them a living and is ethical is useful and important."

90. "It is frightening and satisfying at the same time to think that we shall lose everything we have, including our loved ones – except that to those who believe, death is only a route-way into glory."

91. "Man, apart from God is nothing but meaningless compost."

92. "If you think there is no God, you are lost; if you believe there is no God, you are deceived; and if you know there is no God, you are a fool."

93. "Surely, I said, God's mercies must be new every morning, how else can a repeat-sinner like me find fresh grace to help me live by day by day?"

94. "Don't worry, both Catholics and Protestants will enter Heaven, the irony is, you may be neighbors."

95. "Don't be shocked that homosexuals and molesters are entering Heaven ahead of you,

you spend more time judging them while they were repenting."

96. "There is definitely a Hell, the problem is, if you go there, you will experience it whether you believed it existed or not."

97. "The greatest error of our time is to equate material prosperity with blessings. I don't need to be a believer so that God can bless me with nice things or money or cars or houses or fancy clothes or jewelry, and etc.; I can have all these things without being a believer. However, what I have which is more than material prosperity, is that, for a shameful sinner like me, God's Son died and through His death I have eternal life - that's true prosperity. Some of these preaching material prosperity

messages today, are only concerned with how people will see outside, inside they may be wolves. God does give strength to make wealth, for sure, but wealth is one of the by-products of godliness, not the end of it. I can be prosperous without God (and some wealthiest people on earth have nothing to do with God). Contentment is the greatest mark of godliness. The best way to be rich, anywhere, is (1) hard work (2) sound investing (3) good money-managing skills (4) creativity and (5) discipline, among others. Prosperity which comes by asking for money from people in the name of a cause when that money goes to one's own pocket or account is day-time robbery, and such robbers should be prosecuted on earth, and will have no place in Heaven, for sure."

98. "For anything you contribute a prayer, a thought, money, time, energy or advice to, no matter how the leader wants to take all the credit, God counts you as one of the builders."

99. "There is nothing more valuable on Earth than humans, in Heaven streets are made of gold."

100. "On earth, I have found that there are only two things that matter, God and everything He made; everything else people will force us to buy through ads."

101. "The first best method of truth investigation is through asking questions. In law they call it examination (-in-chief

and cross). The second-best method is through wise anecdotes. Half the world is deceived because it neglects to interrogate its speakers. Truth told is good; truth discovered is even better."

102. "Simply demanding the change of a system without providing alternatives is self-defeatism. Otherwise, we risk replacing thieves with killers."

103. "All humans are born equal – and each individual is given a blank cheque at birth. It is how you think and what you say that either limits or pushes you forward."

104. "You have not conquered the world until you know how to bounce from fear, defeat, shame and disappointment.

After that, you're unstoppable, anywhere on the globe."

105. "Every day is new, literally, so don't transfer yesterday's worries into today. Live as though your yesterday was the worst day of your life; your today as the best day of your life; and your tomorrow has better prospects waiting for you."

106. "Don't say that, 'I want to be better than them all,' rather say, 'I want to be best at what I do.' Do not equally tell your child to be the best at school or college or university, rather ask them to do their best in every class. However hard one may try, there is always someone who will out-do, out-smart or better them in something."

107. "The more I grow the more I realize what truly matters. Family! The time I spend with them matters; the sacrifices I make for them matters; the defence I provide to them matters; the prayers I make for them matters; the wealth I build for them matters; the leadership I provide to them matters; the ___ (fill in the blank) matters."

108. "Everyone who has contributed to my journey of life, even if I can't mention your name, you're my hero. One ought to constantly realize that it is because others stood with them that they are where they are."

109. "Regard no one less than your fainting shadow; strike no one who is already down; before you do or say evil against

another ask: 'I owe every person love; will this pay my full debt?'"

110. "Thoughts are still free – but to set boundaries is the responsibility of men."

111. "The glorious past was framed by men of faith. These men build Harvard and Yale and Princeton prestigious universities. Wisdom is a mark not of intelligence but of faith."

112. "We have not made a legacy until our good works outlive us."

113. "Every time you study, you add an iota of information to your knowledge base; you've sent a statement to your Creator that you appreciate Him for giving you a brain."

114. "All men are created equal – but it is only those who add ideas to skills and to skills action and determination, who reach the top."

115. "The truth about life is that the poor can be rich, and the rich can become poor; and followers can become leaders. But it is travesty when leaders fail to lead."

116. "It is life's greatest regret that one did nothing when they had the chance to do something good."

117. "In the sport of basketball, it is not how many goals you scored that wins you the game, it is how many goals you scored which the other side did not

answer to that wins you the game. In the game of life, it is how many goals you score for others and expect no answer which really matter."

118. "Good and evil are only concepts until you fall and someone else has to pick you up."

119. "Do you know that the one who hates you loves your future, only if you do not retaliate?"

120. "When I saw a corpse (dead body) for the first time, I thought, 'God must have a sense of humor: It cares for nothing it cared most for when it lived.'"

121. "Humility is the safest form of investment; there is no fear

of speculation in it as in the security markets."

122. "Sex, thirst, hunger and sleep have one thing in common; they are not the end but only means to an end."

123. "You're most unsafe and at your weakest point when men praise you, for then you cannot see your own blind spots."

124. "Have you ever noticed that reality shows, day-time TV shows, comedy shows and late-night TV shows all create a fake audience which pander to their interests – the truth is, not everything they applaud to is worth your time; it's all like preaching to the choir."

125. "For long I wondered why God gave us eyes but did not allow us to see our own face, except with the aid of a mirror or through another person. And why we are unable to see our own back (bum) to prevent embarrassment. Then I knew: So that we are not quick to judge others, but quick to realize that we need others."

126. "Risk is heroism, though at the time it may be viewed as a deviation from the norm."

127. "Everyone is sanctimonious at another's funeral; then they understand that life is fragile."

128. "Pride's mightiest fortress is unforgiveness."

129. "Be economical in everything, except with the truth."

130. "If the person you envy is successful, it pains you more and it profits you less to hate them; love them and you will share into their success."

131. "A tree can only be measured after it has fallen; a good man's life is not measured while he lives. Therefore, a person will not escape shame even in the graves."

132. "We can potentially lose everything we love every day; we must practically enjoy everything we love every day."

133. "He who least says 'no' will soon be a slave; and she who always says 'yes' will die young."

134. "All are called to be *in* the world, so engage; but not all are *of* the world, so exercise your right to choose wisely."

135. "A statement ends the thinking; a question extends it."

136. "A statement is like giving someone fish while a question is like giving them a net to fish with!"

137. "It is good to have leaders guiding you; it is better to achieve the same results without a leader guiding you."

138. "Problem with pride is that there is no self-diagnosis – the proud usually think they are so humble that they need to become just a little bit more selfish."

139. "If you are highest in rank among men, you should desire the lowest seat."

140. "The simple test for humility is on the highway – do you think the other motorist you overtake does not deserve to arrive early?"

141. "Pride is ignorance and failure to appreciate that there is someone higher, prettier, stronger, holier, smarter, richer, wiser, tougher, wittier, bigger, smaller, cleaner, thinner, thicker, shorter, taller, more attractive, more handsome, more honest, finer, more special, or plainly better than you are."

142. "The greatest error of our time is to equate material

prosperity with blessings. The two are not the same."

143. "A person can say anything, do anything and think anything in order to be recognized."

144. "It's amazing that in the Garden of Eden, God cursed the ground and other things but not work. He Himself worked, and still works. Work is not cursed. Long time ago I thought only preaching and teaching were serving God. It is only partly true. All and every good work is serving God. Paul says, 'Whatever you do, do all as unto the Lord.' Every secular employment is service to God - when you serve other people, you're serving God. A reward awaits all, whether you served in the Church or on the street. Whatever you are doing right

QUOT-EBOS

now, do it with all your mighty, and enjoy it."

145. "Itch not to hear your fellow brother or sister has fallen, but desire to pray for those who are weak among us."

146. "Be quick to hear of the good fortune of those God has chosen and first to celebrate with those who find favor in Jesus."

147. "If Satan should tempt our leaders to sin and fall, we should all mourn and their burden bear."

148. "Enter business but don't join politics if you want to be rich. Don't use God's pulpit as a fundraiser or as a vehicle to wealth. At the entrance to Hell

the souls you thought you preserved will call for your blood and money will transport you into Hell's fire. Preach Jesus and Him crucified, and if God wills, all other things will be added unto you."

149. "The world has a way of doing things, most of it fun, practical and useful. But the world cannot show the Church how to do things. It is wrong for the Church to start to copy Hollywood style or the world system of endorsement. But the world is still our home while in the flesh, so Christian need to remain relevant to it while not embracing its style. This in itself demands an intricate balance."

150. "I was wondering the meaning of 'Blessing.' If it means money or material possessions only, then I am

doomed, because most people who don't fear God or regard man have more of it. I thought there is more to 'Blessing,' to me it means that I have the peace of, and with, God; to me 'Blessing' means the state of godliness. Some of the most blessed people on earth don't have anything in the bank account."

151. "What Proverbs 3:6 'In all your ways acknowledge him and he will guide you in your ways' does not mean: It does not mean that God will think for you, envision for you and do things for you. God is only your 'guide' or 'director' and he does just that, guide or direct you in a right path/way. It's like a blind man with a guide dog or guide stick; he (the blind man) knows where he is trying to go

but needs the dog or stick to lead (direct) him in the right direction (so that he can arrive with less trouble). That's why God will judge us, he wouldn't have if he thought, dreamed and did things for us."

152. "God and Satan have one thing in common; they both brag about their children. Whose are you?"

153. "The Bible is only a good story book if you read it from cover to cover; a good study text if you analyze it historically; but the Word of God if you meditate on it day and night."

154. "Many a person lives as if there is no God, but wants to die as if they lived for God."

155. "Anything built around the Bible will ultimately stand."

156. "Light breeds responsibility; nations whose light is the Word of God will rule other nations."

157. "Here lies true wisdom: Only that which is founded upon God is truly good."

158. "Those who study the Word of God and live according to its precepts will measure their years in joy; those who don't, in regrets."

159. "Don't live another preacher's dream, for him it is work, for you it is a commitment."

160. "Stop following a church leader who is buying houses and cars using church money.

When the church is broke, he will sell you to the devil."

161. "Turn every woman and man into an instrument of gratitude; aren't you fascinated how your senses react when they pass you by."

162. "Simple people rarely change the world; they fear to disrupt *status quo*."

163. "If you have a dream, even if it is good for all, it will first be opposed by the very people who will eventually benefit from it."

164. "Don't put your trust in a man, however powerful or intelligent he may be; at his weakest moment, he will need your help."

165. "When it comes to your future, you have none, because elsewhere it is already tomorrow."

166. "If dying is like pre-birth, then both the womb and tomb are the same; in both you need someone to care for your soul."

167. "Death is like a shadow; you think you have none until there is light."

168. "Death is like bad breath; the victim is usually the one closest."

169. "Death reveals selfishness' worst moments; everyone thinks today it is another's time, not theirs."

170. "No-one sees themselves when their eyes are closed, and however many hours they spend in front of a mirror making their face up, only another can appreciate how calmly they look."

171. "It is dangerous to take credit for a group project; you might make a lazy member look like a genius."

172. "If you have read a book, you can add up to 100 years to your life; if you have written a book, you can live forever."

173. "It's the responsibility of every human being to care for another human being's responsibility."

174. "Humans are mostly kind and generally behave well one to another when they are

themselves going through hard times."

175. "Every human eventually returns to the soil from whence they came from; the proud pretend they will not rot in their graves."

176. "An oppressor is oppressed by his own heart, the problem is, he doesn't know it."

177. "The gates of Hell open as frequently for the rich nations as the mansions of Heaven are occupied by those from the poor countries."

178. "Perspective matters...I have come to that conclusion, too. Consider that you are a different person from the lenses of your parents (they see you as a fragile little baby), from your

spouses (they see you as a brute, weak and flamboyant hypocrite), from your children (they see you as a flip-flopper, promise-breaker and untrustworthy dictator or listen to them, everything they say about you may be the truth), from your church members (they may see you as a saint, but are you?), from your work-metes (they may see you as lazy, showy and proud morass or happy only on Fridays), from your neighbors (they may see you as a reclusive, materialistic and unhelpful brat or worse) and from yourself (you forget you have tremendous flaws). So, before you over-judge yourself, consider perspective, it matters."'

179. "I prayed not to have everything I wanted but to have all that I needed, lest my sense

of entitlement lead me to forget it was a gift; and to have something, lest my sense of disappointment lead me to steal or insult God."

180. "The single most important revelation of character is that you do not think of yourself higher than you ought to, irrespective of your education, accomplishments or accolades."

181. "Don't underestimate love for self – it can kill father, marry mother, sell siblings and curse God."

182. "Rejection is like an infection; it does not go away without treatment."

183. "Accept every human being but reject their encumbrances."

184. "Sometimes the greatest escape to freedom and happiness is in the simple statement: 'I don't care what people are going to say.'"

185. "People are nothing but dust and food for warms, until they do something that has everlasting worth."

186. "You can determine how you want to be remembered."

187. "Don't enjoy another person's work without acknowledging they did it, and not you."

188. "Don't envy another person's calling, each person's calling is as distinctive as a fork is from a garden rake."

189. "Saying 'No' can be the difference between life and

death, freedom and bondage, love and hate and wellness and sickness. There are more 'Yes' on many graves than there are 'Nos'. Learning to say 'No' can protect you, evade danger and elude peril because it takes courage and thought to say 'No' rather than 'Yes'. Most people are in problems just because they said, 'Yes' when they should have said 'No.'' It's better to say 'No' and be hated for it but be safe and free, than say 'Yes' and be liked for it but be in danger and bondage forever."

190. "Twelve good reasons to be at your best in any given year: (1) Set a goal and begin to pursue it right from January 1st; (2) learn from your failures of the previous year; focus on what made you succeed; (3)

think like a winner even when failure stares you in your face; (4) wear confidence throughout the year, even when you dream; (5) make God first, family second and everything else last; (6) don't ever worry about anything, even when tempted to do so; (7) believe you can do and achieve, anything you've set your mind to do; (8) avoid idle moments; make every second count for something valuable; (9) don't drudge; enjoy your work and find good time to eat, love, and pray; (10) don't use all the money you make; invest and save as much; (11) give more than you will receive; and (12) believe you are (smart; kind; handsome/beautiful; able; humble; strong and etc.) best at what you are."

191. "No matter how rich you are, you have only one mouth and only one stomach."

192. "Now I know that no-one can know God except under two uncommon conditions: When one walks with Him in shame, pain, suffering, disappointments, misery, rejection, failure, and total loss of everything; and the other, through sheer grace – God's free and unmerited favor."

193. "What if you had nothing – no food, no home, no car, no money, no clothes, no shoes, no influence, no position, no name to defend, no-one to love you, no survival scheme, no job and no education or any achievements – would you still love and praise God?"

194. "If you don't become what you thought you would be, become what God thinks of you and just be."

195. "Anything or anyone you are fighting for ask: Will the success of the mission be called by its or their name, or will it be eternally a dedication either to the people as a whole or to God? If it falls short of these two, you are wasting your time."

196. "The Bible doesn't say that the devil doesn't know the truth; he does. He even believes the truth, but trembles. The truth is, he manipulates the truth in order to sustain his real nature, a lying."

197. "He is a wise person who recognizes that it is not bad to enjoy life; he who loves God

must also love what God created."

198. "The same John who wrote, 'Do not love the world or the things that are in the world,' also wrote 'For God so loved the world that He gave His only begotten Son…'"

199. "When I die, I will have only one hope: That what I believed was true, that Christ had forgiven and forgotten all my faults, and that though surprised and shocked, I will join the throng of all the faithful who in the unseen God had placed all their trust, on earth, like I did."

200. "Only God can make dust like me eat, laugh, merry and give Him praise."

201. "I would rather be in the company of my family with Christ spend my Sunday, than in a Church congregation full of the glory and story of men accompanied by self-adorations called praise and ad-formulations called testimony be."

202. "As this year comes to an end, I think, sadly, about the Church's inability to creatively reach the people who need the Gospel most. Ministers of Gospel are now greedy beasts, womanizers and plainly 'robbers.' Congregations now compete against each other on who has the best buildings, cars or women. And the Church now preaches more condemnatory sermons than grace. And few people are accepted in these 'churches' because of favoritism and

judgmentalism. Some pastors are now the worst unforgivers (some will not even hide that they hate you, especially if you challenge their appetites for gain at the expense of the poor in the name of God). Christians now behave more wickedly than non-believers (sometimes a non-believer can be honest with you; believers will ostracize you without shame). And everyone forgets that Jesus ate with 'sinners,' and all his disciples had several flaws and yet Jesus accepted them just the way they were. If the Church continues on this trajectory next year, it is going to be an instrument of destruction and not of hope and salvation. God forbid that mammon should be elevated in pulpits at the expense of Jehovah. God forbids that pride should rule at the expense of humility. God forbids that hate should reign at the expense of love. Let us be honest. Let everyone judge their motives. God cannot be fooled. What I am saying is that we should rather have Jesus than religion."

203. "I looked at the window and saw the grandeur and magnificence of a modern building structure, and thought, 'God can push it all just with a pinky of his finger and it is all uprooted from the base,' then I thought, 'How tiny relative to man is an ant, yet it builds quite the same as humans do,' then I concluded: 'Surely, humans are just as ants in the eyes of God, yet He calls them His children and cares for them more – how special they must be. Yet, still, they are just a little bit better than insects."

204. "If you believe that all that die go to Heaven, you have faith big enough to move mountains."

205. "Men look at the complete structure and say, 'A house'; God looks at individual bricks and say, 'My house."

206. "Blessings do come through rough roads, painful pangs, failed missions, disappointing projects, and stressful seasons. When something bad happens to you, it is usually because something truly good is about to happen, and it will happen."

207. "Do not live through a calamity before it happens; do not stay in a calamity once it happens; and do not dwell on

the effects of the calamity after it has happened."

208. "There is no road that leads to nowhere."

209. "In the road to progress, there will be a Mary that will care for you; a John that will love you; a Peter that will deny you; a Judas that will betray you; a Thomas that will doubt you; a soldier that will believe in you; a brother that will despise you; a Nicodemus that will follow you secretly; a Zacchaeus that will support you; a majority that will do nothing; and God who will sustain you."

210. "If someone reaches out their hand as a friend, shack it; if, however, they reach it out as an enemy, cut it off," (Turkish Saying).

211. "If you befriend a bear, it will eat you when it is hungry," (Turkish Saying).

212. "Have the ears of an owl and the eyes of a falcon."

213. "What you compliment lives; what you criticize dies."

214. "So long as there is breath in me, that long will I persist. For now, I know one of the greatest principles of success; if I persist long enough, I will win," (OG Mandino).

215. "A smile conquers your heart before it gives you entrance into that of another."

216. "The Orbit Principle is based on a very simple fact that: Whatever a man sows, that he will also reap."

217. "When a farmer perceives that a tree does not live up to its potential, he may prune in to allow it to produce more."

218. "You don't need to be academically correct in your definition of integrity."

219. "It pays to use the brain."

220. "Everything we see and use around us is virtually someone else's idea that became a reality."

221. "The trouble with most people is that they rarely make use of their ideas."

222. "Society only responds to how much you allow it to limit you."

223. "I was bored enough to refuse to listen to the voice of 'what ifs' in order to spend time writing something you might be finding helpful right now."

224. "In the leadership race, the way you finish is more important than the way you began."

225. "One thing society has not done is to fail to inform us about men and women who endured tests, narrowly escaped death, sacrificed all for the human cause, were imprisoned for standing up for the truth, dared not to give up hope when that hope meant the freedom of many people, and the list is endless."

226. "Freedom from self-pity will enable you to take

responsibility both for your own failure and success."

227. "Self-pity is the world's worst emotion."

228. "Don't send your prayers to an unknown god."

229. "'Sleep on it,' a good night rest will double your chances of finding a creative solution to your problems."

230. "Some people are made by circumstances; others use circumstances to their advantage. We call the later enthusiasts."

231. "In leadership enthusiasm is not only an asset, but it is also the engine that propels the leadership machine. An enthusiastic leader will inspire his or her people to carry-on

even when failure is staring them in the face."

232. "I know you have a dream. I will only urge you to do one thing, be enthusiastic."

233. "Frank, the father of Belinda Stronach, believed he could make it in the automotive industry when he found a job, got fired, saved enough money to take a bus to Kitchener, Ontario, Canada where he begged for a job that eventually gave him enough money to buy a tool kit to start his own company, Magna International Inc., the multibillion-dollar automotive-parts company."

234. "'I Can,' the world's best two English words."

235. "Fear is never free."

236. "Failure is not final," (Joe Imakando).

237. "Thoughts are free," (Munyonzwe Hamalengwa).

238. "One's youthfulness, is their greatest natural resource."

239. "Harvey Weinstein, an American former film producer and convicted sex offender, was at the center of many Hollywood movies with overt sexual overtures and unfettered lewd language; doesn't this explain why Hollywood movies have brought the world closer to Hell than Heaven?"

240. "Guard your sense of self-respect; it'll protect your life's greatest human endowments."

241. "An excuse is the world's most crippling disease."

242. "You are the most important person in the world, simply let your character match it."

243. "Satan likes people who read about prayer; loves people who hate prayer; hates people who know the power of prayer; but only fears the people who pray."

244. "Every parent has a responsibility to pray for their family, daily, if possible."

245. "Teach people how to pray for others, they will automatically learn how to pray for themselves."

246. "Prayer is like an exercise (gym) - everyone knows it is good, but very few find time to do it."

247. "Prayer and peace are like a person and their shadow; where one is the other follows."

248. "You cannot hate who you pray for."

249. "When prayer intrudes into worry, worry is converted into peace."

250. "Prayer is the only key that opens doors locked from the inside."

251. "Prayer is the ladder we use if we want to access our heavenly investments."

252. "I know that every prayer I pray will be answered; only that it can be 'yes' or 'no.'"

253. "Sometimes prayer is the highest revelation of the selfishness in our hearts; that is why it purifies the soul."

254. "I hope for my people Zambians and Canadians that they will trust each other, see one another as friends and equals, respect their respective value systems, practice reciprocity in national investments and support each other within their sovereign bounds."

255. "Africa – it is profitless to brag about your abundant natural resources if you can't manipulate them into prosperity and development; it is equally

counterproductive if the only benefit you derive from your resources is forex."

256. "If I were to be born again, I would still choose to be born Black; because Black loves black, white, brown and yellow."

257. "If America and Europe are smart, it will be a catastrophic error to undervalue Africa."

258. "I have represented clients of all races on earth and I am heartened to know that they are all fine human beings."

259. "Do not generalize the badness of one person to the entire race, tribe or caste; particularize the endearment of one person to all she is and does."

260. "Zambia, you can walk into prosperity if you do five simple things: Produce; prioritize; plow back; professionalize; and profitize."

261. "It is amazing that in the Christian Bible, God commands all inanimate created things to praise Him, but he gives it as an option to humanity to praise Him."

262. "Don't be surprised to find out that God loves even those whom you may hate."

263. "Whenever there is a need, grace shows up to lighten the burden."

264. "Grace shines like a tintless shining glass."

265. "Although mercy may not always be accompanied by grace, grace is always accompanied by mercy."

266. "What makes grace amazing is in the fact that right takes the punishment that wrong deserves and wrong is rewarded with the good that bad does deserve."

267. "Grace is like seasoning – to be effective, it must filer through and marinate the entire behavior."

268. "The difference between love and grace is their similarity."

269. "Grace is divine nature resident in frail human life."

270. "Love hugs the prisoner; truth sets the prisoner's

conscience free; mercy unshackles the prisoner's chains; righteousness changes his corrupt garments; justice breaks the prison bars; and grace rewards the freed prisoner with lasting benefits he did not deserve."

271. "Grace is thinner than ice and lighter than air."

272. "In relations, grace is a diplomat; in languages, grace is a finesse speaker; in fashion, grace is a moderate designer; in competition, grace is a fair umpire; and in industry, grace is the formidable refiner."

273. "Grace is the last stage of human perfection."

274. "Even when he executes the law, a gracious leader is merciful."

275. "Grace is the highest state of excellence, and the highest form of morality."

276. "Where there is virtue, there is no law; but where there is grace, the law is powerless."

277. "Where there is grace, love is perfected."

278. "Grace smoothens social edges and oils human blunts."

279. "Grace and evil are inversely related; the more one increases, the less one reduces."

280. "Grace on human behavior, has the same effect as beauty has on a human psyche."

281. "Love, faith and hope are all subsets of grace; he who has them all, has the complete set."

282. "She who is gracious, has great love and is rich in mercy."

283. "Love and compassion are two sides of a gracious coin."

284. "Under grace, suffering always leads to glory."

285. "Grace is a reset button on a restoration garget."

286. "Grace calls those things that have done nothing as if they have done everything."

287. "If you are too quick to get angry, you have a deficiency in the grace hormone."

288. "In the grace gymnasium, patience is the equipment that builds muscles."

289. "If you forgive others, you are a student of grace even if you missed registration."

290. "Sin is the sjambok that law uses to inflict chagrin on those who dwell outside the realm of grace."

291. "I love the God of the New Testament – because there is nothing that you can do or fail to do, good or bad, right or wrong, darling or weird, lovely or hateful, happily or woefully, that can separate you from His love."

292. "The power to say 'No' to evil resides in grace."

293. "Be nice to others, and even nicer to yourself."

294. "Let kindness and compassion be your default position."

295. "GRACE – Goodness, righteousness and cheerfulness endear."

296. "Finally, brothers, whatever is true, whatever is noble, whatever is right, whatever is pure, whatever is lovely, whatever is admirable--if anything is excellent or praiseworthy--think about such things," (Philippians 4:8, Bible).

ABOUT THE AUTHOR

CHARLES MWEWA

Charles Mwewa (LLM – cand.) is a Dad, a husband, a prolific author and researcher, poet, novelist, political thinker, a law professor, and Christian and community leader. Mwewa has written no less than 30 books and counting. Mwewa, his wife and their three daughters, reside in the Canadian Capital City of Ottawa.

AUTHOR'S CONTACT

Email address:
spynovel2016@gmail.com

Facebook:
www.facebook.com/charlesmwewa

Twitter:
https://twitter.com/BooksMwewa

Instagram:
www.instagram.com/mwewabooks/?hl=en

Author's website:
https://www.charlesmwewa.com

To order this book online:

https://www.amazon.com/dp/1988251257

INDEX

A

abomination, 57
abuse, 86, 232
accolades, 105, 267
accomplishments, 15
achievement, 35, 105, 108, 111
acquit, 55
action, 14
Adam, 135, 180, 228
Adam and Eve, 135, 228
adulthood, 83
adversity, 43
advocate, 142
Africa, 27
African, 1
al-Qaeda, 234
al-Shabaab, 234
American, 1
anger, 207
answer, 26
ants, 95
apartheid, 59
appoint yourself, 28
attracting, 12
Attraction v. Attitude, 10

B

bad breath, 263
balance, 47, 56, 68, 143, 185, 258
basketball, 249
bear, 141, 211, 257
beauty, 33, 125, 131, 153, 168, 171, 173, 174, 189, 292

betrayal, 46, 48, 62
Bible, 82, 117, 129, 174, 204, 260
birth, 29
bitterness, 81
blessings, 89, 90, 111, 146, 159, 256
blind man, 259
blind people, 4
blind spots, 251
body, 22
Boko Haram, 234, 235
born, 8
boss, 166, 187
brain, 22, 24, 28, 195, 198, 248
brave, 51, 218
buffalo, 211
Build a System, 5
Build the Structure, 5
bulls, 9
business, 45, 110

C

calamity, 30
captain, 3
care, 9, 10, 13, 67, 71, 97, 149, 170, 185, 184, 220, 233, 234, 263, 264, 268
career, 40, 110, 178, 193, 240
category of followers, 97
Catholics, 241
cats, 213
champion, 102, 167
chance, 223
character, 39
characteristics of caring

leadership, 101
child, 111, 123, 128, 133, 135, 149, 189, 246
childhood, 83
Christ, 40, 73, 117, 141, 142, 143, 145, 172, 184
Christian, 92, 174
Christopher Columbus, 92
church, 99, 141, 146, 172, 181, 184, 185, 261
citizens, 61, 62, 79, 91
coach, 99
collateral damage, 60
commander, 99
commissions, 208
compassion, 40
compost, 241
confidence, 8, 94, 173, 191, 225
conquer, 7
conscience, 58
constitution, 7, 58, 86
contribution, 101
Coronavirus, 79
corruption, 56, 89, 220
country, 1
courage, 3
Covid-19, 77, 78, 79
Creator, 71, 185, 238, 248
credit, 76, 244, 264
criticisms, 8
culture, 1
customers, 223
customs, 162

D

darkest, 38
Day of Judgment, 205
deacon, 99
dead body, 250
death, 38, 57, 62, 93, 163, 167, 170, 188, 179, 181, 182, 195, 235, 240
debt, 248
decisions, 8
defeat, 30, 37, 46, 77, 163, 218, 245
delegation, 93
desire, 32
devil, 13, 53, 117, 142, 146, 225, 228, 262
disabilities, 43
disappointment, 73, 193, 245, 267
disappointments, 37
discipline, 24, 41, 88, 97, 98, 133, 189, 243
discouragements, 39
discriminate, 56, 103, 212
disobedience, 63
divorce, 174
dogs, 31, 212
dollars, 12, 106, 111
dream, 5

E

eagle, 212
earth, 21
education, 99, 184, 267

elder, 99
elephants, 211
emergency, 93
ends-in-mind, 3
enemy, 30, 40, 41, 48, 78, 151, 188, 217, 218, 219, 228, 235
equality, 61
equitable, 61
equity, 61, 66
error, 255
ethical standards, 92
Europe, 29
European, 1
Eve, 135
evidence, 54, 55, 142, 143
exam, 23
examination, 244
excellence, 2
exclusionism, 59
eyes, 8

F

failure, 10, 11, 14, 35, 45, 46, 73, 76, 82, 144, 151, 193, 223, 233, 255
faith, 8, 25, 41, 81, 92, 94, 139, 145, 146, 188, 180, 182, 183, 200, 203, 225, 248
faithfulness, 50
family, 78, 137, 146, 175, 186, 190, 212, 225, 247, 270, 274, 285

favor, 43, 68, 73, 150, 212, 257
favoritism, 66
fear, 40, 46, 73, 76, 77, 81, 117, 198, 245, 250, 259, 262
financial model, 110
fire, 38
first, 22
focus, 7
followers, 3
fool, 26
foolishness, 14, 31, 32, 189
Four Pillars of a Vision, 4
fox, 213
fraudsters, 78
freedom, 57, 103, 221, 268
friendship, 48, 67, 68
funeral, 15, 252
future, 2, 6, 7, 26, 29, 32, 43, 90, 125, 127, 140, 179, 180, 182, 184, 186, 189, 221, 250, 263

G

gazelle, 213
geese, 213
general, 93, 99, 218
genitalia, 33, 81, 186
gentleness, 50
goals, 1
goats, 9, 96
God, 2, 7, 22, 26, 29, 31, 32, 33, 37, 38, 40, 42,

48, 49, 50, 57, 58, 60,
62, 63, 64, 65, 73, 77,
79, 89, 90, 92, 108, 117,
127, 135, 137, 138, 140,
141, 143, 144, 145, 146,
147, 150, 163, 166, 172,
173, 180, 185, 186, 188,
183, 185, 186, 188, 191,
192, 193, 194, 195, 196,
197, 202, 203, 204, 206,
207, 225, 228, 229, 230,
231, 237, 241, 244, 250,
257, 259, 260, 261, 267
gold, 25, 126, 133, 161,
162, 180, 181, 225, 244
golden rule, 78
good and evil, 250
goodness, 50
government, 53, 54, 62, 63,
79, 90, 91, 92, 112
governor, 62, 99
governors, 53, 57
grace, 8, 49, 58, 85, 94,
117, 138, 168, 238, 241
graves, 253, 265
greatness, 43

H

Half-full v. Half-empty Attitude,
11
happiness, 107, 112, 160,
172, 268
happy, 54, 112, 151, 181,
187, 218, 227
hard times, 265
hard work, 90, 150, 161

hardships, 35
Harvard, 248
hate evil, 55
heart, 4, 22, 26, 27, 47, 65,
71, 92, 135, 138, 140,
144, 146, 160, 162, 163,
165, 171, 172, 175, 188,
195, 209, 219, 221, 229,
239, 265
Heaven, 21
Hell, 27, 242, 257, 265
heroism, 187, 252
hindrance, 40
history, 43
Hollywood, 258
homosexuals, 241
hope, 111, 140, 166, 181,
187, 179, 180, 181, 182,
183, 184, 185, 186, 187,
188, 189, 190, 191, 198
hope and a future, 191
hopelessness, 40
horses, 10
human rights, 60, 63
humility, 234, 255
hungry, 206
hypocrisy, 146, 202

I

I can succeed, 226
ideas, 16, 24, 75, 76, 110,
193, 196, 212, 249
If I fail, 226
ignorance, 22
implementation, 190
important, 13

impossible, 228
injury, **59**, 60
injustice, **59**, 60, 62, 66, 238
instructor, **99**
instrument of gratitude, **262**
integrity, **89**, 183
intellectual genius, **92**
intercession, **137**, 138
investigators, **167**
invincible, **30**

J

Jesus, **32**
job, **37**
journey, **12**, 81, 106, 111, 168, 191, 247
joy, **38**, 50, 65, 73, 117, 217, 261
judge, **54**, 55, 59, 85, 142, 180, 260
judgment, **13**
justice, **53**, 55, 58, 65, 66

K

kindness, **50**
King David, **135**, 194
know, **9**
knowledge, **4**

L

labyrinth, **86**

laugh, **36**, 222
law, **53**, 54, 56, 57, 58, 59, 61
law of importunity, **192**
lawyer, **142**, 175
laziness, **125**, 192, 220, 226, 228
lazy, **47**, 112, 125, 177, 228, 264
leaders, **4**
leadership, **1**
leadership dynamics, **96**
leads by example, **102**
liberty, **221**
life, **35**
life is fragile, **252**
lifestyle, **42**
light, **24**, 64, 66, 101, 131, 188, 202, 261, 263
limit, **7**
losers, **13**
love, **49**, 51, 150, 159, 160, 161, 162, 163, 164, 165, 166, 167, 168, 169, 170, 171, 175, 201

M

management, **2**
mandate, **86**
marriage, **150**
marry, **25**
master, **27**, 99, 160, 166, 167, 183, 205, 238
mayor, **99**

mercy, 40, 62, 63, 85, 147, 150, 159, 164
millionaires, 228
mind, 2
mindset, 4
ministry, 146
miracles, 37
misunderstandings, 32
mockery, 206
molesters, 241
money, 26, 69, 75, 76, 78, 90, 103, 104, 105, 106, 108, 109, 110, 111, 112, 113, 146, 177, 188, 181, 184, 192, 193, 244, 258, 261
morality, 55, 60, 85, 89
motivation, 224, 235
mountains, 8, 187

N

naked, 32
nations, 31
nature, 22
neighbor, 57, 77, 79, 151, 160, 166, 227
Nelson Mandela, 45
nobility, 205

O

obstacles, 3, 50, 230
ocean, 21
omissions, 208
open mouth, 32

operations, 2
oppressor, 265
organization, 3
ownership of success and failure, 96

P

pain, 40, 49, 68, 73, 82, 164, 180, 217, 230
pandemic, 77, 78, 79
parent, 99, 137
partner, 32
past, 13, 43, 92, 117, 127, 179, 180, 186, 248
pastor, 99, 146, 172, 181
patience, 39, 50, 169, 171, 217
Paul, 135
peace, 50, 81, 111, 137, 140, 143, 219, 259
perception, 12, 115
perfection, 35
perish, 15
persistence, 36
perspective, 24, 45
petitions, 143
philosophies, 42
policy, 89
politics, 99, 135, 257
poor countries, 265
positions, 7
positive expectation, 190
potential, 22
poverty, 63, 112
power, 42
power, 86, 135

praise, 41
prayer, 135, 137, 138, 140, 141, 143, 144
preaching to the choir, 251
president, 99, 186, 235
presidents, 4
pride, 252, 255
prime minister, 99
Princeton, 248
principle, 11, 108, 151
prisoner, 173
problem-solving, 94
procrastinating, 76
productivity, 220
profession, 25
professional, 47, 178
professor, 99, 234
profit, 106, 107, 253
prognostication, 196
progress, 21
promise, 39
promotion, 37
prosperity, 31, 56, 82, 92, 256
Protestants, 241
proverbs, 259
psychological impact, 106
punishment, 38

Q

question, 254
quit, 12

R

race, 1, 35, 45, 68, 172, 201, 238
racism, 59
reality, 2, 188, 251
re-cycle, 231
refuse, 12
rejection, 68
relationship, 143, 149, 152, 171, 172, 174, 176, 177, 225
religion, 41, 150, 234, 238
resistance, 36
restraint, 86, 133
retaliate, 250
re-use, 231
revelation, 29
rich nations, 103, 265
riches, 112, 187
righteousness, 60, 62, 66, 206
rule of love, 152, 153, 154, 155, 156, 157
rule of power, 86
rules, 85, 166, 224

S

salvation, 25, 145, 203
Satan, 42
scriptures, 32, 203
seasons, 236
secrets, 29
self-control, 50, 169

self-diagnosis, 254
selfish, 151, 254
self-respect, 36
separation, 50
seven billion people, 14
sex, 27, 29, 68, 107, 171,
  176, 177, 178, 179, 180,
  181, 183, 184, 186, 187,
  251
shadow, 137, 188, 247, 263
sheep, 9
shepherd, 7
silence, 43
sin, 41, 57, 60, 62, 135,
  150, 228, 257
skillset, 5
slavery, 191
smile, 41
social distance,, 77
social media, 110
solution, 8
speculation, 251
Speculation v. Anticipation, 10
speech, 207
spiritual success, 145
spouse, 26, 32, 61, 149,
  151, 172, 173
spring, 36
statement, 248, 254, 268
status, 1
strategy and tactics, 224
strength, 11
struggle, 104, 105, 146,
  221, 229
student, 23
submissive woman, 221
succeed, 16

success, 10, 14, 44, 45, 76,
  82, 96, 108, 118, 198,
  222, 223, 230, 234, 253
suffering, 49, 73
supplications, 143
sweetness, 81

T

tastes, 47
teacher, 10
teamwork, 95
thank you, 223
thanksgiving, 143
think, 9
time, 197, 199
today, 13, 15, 199, 232,
  239, 246, 263
traditions, 42
trainer, 99
trap, 42
treasure, 68, 81
tree, 17, 253
trouble, 30
true friend, 67, 68, 71
Trump, 79
trust, 73, 129, 144, 185,
  186, 262
truth, 32, 42, 49, 66, 73,
  141, 165, 236, 244, 249,
  251, 252
trying again, 223
tyranny, 85

U

unanswered prayer, 147
unfailing love, 184
unforgiveness, 252
universe, 6

V

value, 27
victim, 263
victory, 31
vision, 2
visionary, 1, 50

W

war, 29
weakest point, 251
weakness, 36
wealth, 111, 127, 222, 247, 257
weapon, 32, 33, 53, 169, 176, 177, 179
weapons, 30
whip, 190

win, 42
windows, 8
winner, 167
winter, 36
Win-Win v. Win-Lose Attitude, 10
wisdom, 8, 47, 65, 92, 94, 113, 183, 202, 207, 261
wise person, 30
word, 92, 143, 184, 260, 261
worry, 23, 140, 241
worship, 143

X

xenophobia, 59

Y

Yale, 248

Z

zero, 23, 197

www.ingramcontent.com/pod-product-compliance
Lightning Source LLC
Chambersburg PA
CBHW060455090426
42735CB00011B/1996